Bhajanamritam

Devotional songs of
Sri Mata Amritanandamayi

I0142925

Volume 6

Mata Amritanandamayi Center
San Ramon, California, United States

Bhajanamritam
Volume 6

Published by:
Mata Amritanandamayi Center
P.O. Box 613
San Ramon, CA 94583-0613
USA

In India:
www.amritapuri.org
inform@amritapuri.org

In USA:
www.amma.org

In Europe:
www.amma-europe.org

Contents

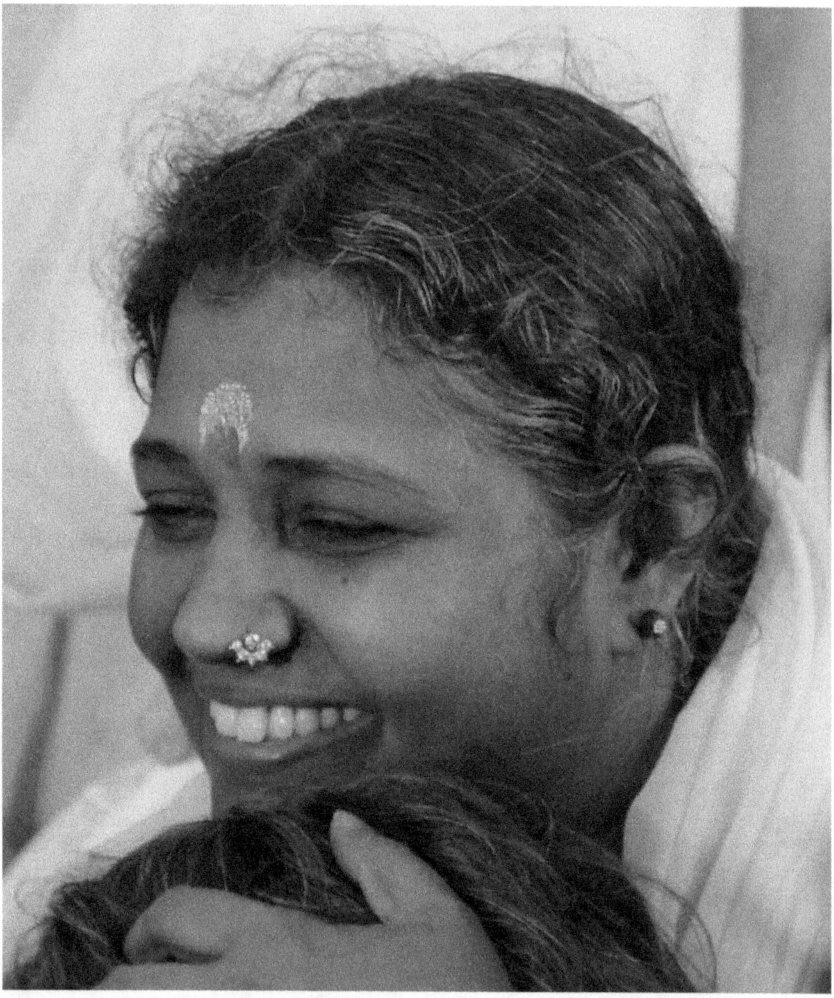

About Pronunciation

The following key is for the guidance of those who are unfamiliar with the Sanskrit and Malayalam transliteration codes which are used in this book:

A	-as	a	in America
AI	-as	ai	in aisle
AU	-as	ow	in how
E	-as	e	in they
I	-as	ea	in heat
O	-as	o	in or
U	-as	u	in suit
KH	-as	kh	in Eckhart
G	-as	g	in give
GH	-as	gh	in loghouse
PH	-as	ph	in shepherd
BH	-as	bh	in clubhouse
TH	-as	th	in lighthouse
DH	-as	dh	in redhead
C	-as	c	in cello
CH	-as	ch-h	in staunch-heart
JH	-as	dge	in hedgehog
Ñ	-as	ny	in canyon
Ś	-as	sh	in shine
Ṣ	-as	c	in efficient
Ṅ	-as	ng	in sing, (nasal sound)
V	-as	v	in valley, but closer to a "w"
ZH	-as	rh	in rhythm

Vowels which have a line on top of them are long vowels, they are pronounced like the vowels listed above but are held for twice the amount of time.
The letters with dots under them (ṭ, ṭh, ḍ, ḍh, ṇ, l, ṣ) are palatal consonants, they are pronounced with the tip of the tongue against the hard palate. Letters without such dots are dental consonants and are pronounced with the tongue against the base of the teeth.

Bhajans

ABHIVANDANAM (TELUGU)

abhivandanam abhivandanam
ādi gaṇapati nīku abhivandanam

Salutations to Ganapati, the primordial one.

jagadamba oṭilōna gārālu kuṭicēṭṭi
bāla gaṇapati nīku abhivandanam
muddu cūpulatōṭa mahēśu nalariñcu
prathama gaṇapati nīku abhivandanam

Salutations to the child Ganapati, who is pampered in the lap of Jagadamba, Mother of the universe. Salutations to Ganapati who makes Lord Shiva happy by his sweet glances.

vātsalya bhāvāna ṣaṇmukhuni tilakiñcu
vighna dēvara nīku abhivandanam
callani cūpulatō lōkāla nēlēṭṭi
vijaya gaṇapati nīku abhivandanam

Salutations to Ganesha, remover of obstacles, who looks at Shanmukha with compassion. Salutations to victorious Ganapati who rules over all the worlds with kindness.

buddhi siddhula gūrcu ā vakratuṇḍunaku
vighnamula parimārcu ā amba sutunaku
siddhidvāramunēlu mūla gaṇapati nīku
bhakti mirage cētu ātmābhivandanam

Salutations to the Lord with a curved trunk, who bestows knowledge and power. Salutations to the son of the Divine Mother who removes obstacles.

ĀDIPARAMA JYŌTIVAI (TELUGU)

ādiparama jyōtivai
ādi pranava nādamai
śakala jīvula jīvamai
veligē daivamā

O Supreme effulgence, who manifests as the primordial light. You are the pranava sound (om) and the life of all existence.

nā jīvana prāṇamā
sakala bhuvana tējamā
ālakiñcu nā vēdana
akhila lōka pālanā

O my life's Life, illumination of the world, listen to my painful cry! O ruler of the world!

chitta dōṣālē māpu
vivēka kānti dīpamā
nā jīvana chukkānivai
dāri chūpi nadipimppumā
rāvegā nā prāṇa dīpamā
māyagā nā bhāva timiramu
chērchukō nī pāda sannidhinē

You are the discriminative light that removes the wrong notions of the mind. Be my life's pole star, showing me the way. Come soon, O light of my life! Dispelling the darkness of the notion of "I", take me to Your lotus feet.

māya jagati tāpame
śamiñchu malaya pavanamā
nā prema pārijātamai
prakaṭiñchi pravahimppumā
rāvegā nā prāṇa dīpamā
māyagā nā bhāva timiramu
chērchukō nī pāda sannidhinē

You are the cool breeze that pacifies the heat of the illusory world; manifest as my unfading, fragrant love and flow through me. Come soon, O light of my life! Dispelling the darkness of the notion of "I", take me to Your lotus feet.

Ā-Ī BHAVĀNĪ (MARATHI)

ā-ī bhavānī ānandadāyinī
aṣṭabhujā tū simhavāhinī
bhaktavalsalē pāpanāśinī
namana tulā hē tuḷjābhavānī

O Mother Bhavani, giver of bliss! You have eight hands and ride a lion. You are the loving mother of the devotees, the destroyer of sin. You reside at Tuljapur, O Mother, our salutations to You!

ā-ī ude ude g ambā-bā-ī

Victory, victory to the divine Mother!

mahālakṣmi karavīravāsini
jagadambā ramā nārāyaṇī
ādimāyā tū jagajananī
namana tulā hē viṣṇuvilāsinī

Goddess of wealth residing at Karavir, Mother of the universe, Rama, Narayani. You are the primordial power, Mother of all the worlds. You delight Lord Vishnu, our salutations to You!

ā-ī rēṇukā parama paravanī
ānandarūpīnī māhūravāsinī
ēkavīrā tū bhavabhayahāriṇī
namana tulā hē bhārgavajananī

Mother Renuka, supreme one, You are the power behind speech. Bestower of bliss, You reside at Mahur. O Ekavira, You remove the fear of the unknown. Mother of Bhargava, our salutations to You!

ādiśakti saptaśrngavāsinī
kalimalahāriṇi āsuramardini
viśvapālike mahāyōginī
namana tulā hē vaṇībhavānī

You are the primordial power, residing at Saptasringi. You remove the fear of death, and destroy all demons. You are the support of the universe, supreme ascetic, Goddess of speech - our salutations to You!

prēmasvarūpiṇi mangalakāriṇī
śāntādurgā umā śivānī
jagajananī akhilasvarūpiṇī
namana tulā hē bhavatāriṇī

Embodiment of love, cause of auspicious deeds, Shantadurga, Uma, Shivani. Mother of the universe, omnipresent one who helps us cross the ocean of birth and death, our salutations to You!

AJNABI RĀH KĒ (HINDI)

ajnabi rāh kē ajnabi rāsatē
phir bhi caltē rahē ik tērē vāstē
bīc sāgar mē hun mai kinārānahī
kōyī sāthī nahī kōyī sahārā nahī
phir bhi caltē rahē ik tērē vāstē
mā ō mā ō mā ō mā

O Mother, we travel an unknown path, in an unknown direction, but we keep on walking, just for You. We are lost in the middle of the ocean, and we cannot find the shore. We have no friend, no support, but we continue on, only to reach You. O Mother, O Mother, O Mother.

dard sīnē mē lēkar bhaṭaktē rahē
har kadam par uṭkar girtē rahē
phirbhi manmē ās lēkē caldiyē
antamē tērē caraṇōmē ā paṭē
mā ō mā ō mā ō mā

We roam helplessly, with aching hearts. We fall with every step, but still we keep moving forward. With hope in our hearts, we keep walking. We know, at the end, we will find refuge in Your lotus feet. O Mother, O Mother, O Mother.

āvāz dēkar diltumē bulārahā ō mā
jō dardthā miṭgayā nā gilā rahā ō mā
tērē yād mē āsū yē bahē
chūṭhēna tērāsath jabtak yē dam rahē – (2)
mā ō mā ō mā ō mā

O Mother, our hearts are calling You. Whatever pain we once felt has vanished, along with our complaints. May we shed tears in Your remembrance: until our last breath, we wish only to stay close to You. O Mother, O Mother, O Mother.

AKAMANATIN KĀRIRUḶAI (TAMIL)

akamanatin kāriruḷai
nīkkiṭumun pēraruḷai
nānmaraiyin nar poruḷai
nāṭivantēn nānumammā
pāvaminta ezhaiyammā

Your grace removes the dark clouds within. I have come in search of she who is the essence of the four Vedas

saraṇam saraṇam kāḷiyamma
saranam durgā dēviyamma

I surrender to Mother Kali, I surrender to Durga Devi!

puviyālum punnakaiyarasi
putirnirainta bhuvanamitil
aruḷnirai attiruvaṭiyil
manam kuvintiṭa vēṇḍumammā – en
manam kuvintiṭa vēṇḍumammā

You have a captivating smile, and You are the one who rules this universe full of puzzles. Let my mind be fully focused on Your lotus feet that are full of grace.

tuyarkaḷ nirainta vaiyakattil
tumbakkaṭalil mūzhgukirēn
maraikaḷ pottrum nāyakiyē
piḷḷaiyenai kāppāye - piḷḷaiyenai kāppāye

The world is full of sorrow- I am drowning in the sea of sadness. You who have been praised in all the four Vedas- please come and save this child of Yours!

ĀLAMBAHĪNA (MALAYALAM)

ālambahīnarkkorattāṇiyānū nī,
āgamōdyāna sugandham!
ātmasvātantryābhi vāṇcchitarkkamma nī
bhāvanātītāvabōdham!

You are the support for the destitutes, the fragrance of garden of scriptures. Amma, You are the unimaginable insight for those who wish for the freedom of soul.

pūmaṇam pēṛunna kāttupōl īśvarā
dēśangaḷ nīḷepparatti,
pārinnatirvarampillāte pāyunna
kāruṇya 'svargamga'yamma!

Like the breeze carries the fragrance all around the nations, Mother is the compassion of "Swarganga"(the Ganges in heaven) which flows without any boundaries.

randakṣaramkondu jīvalōkattinde
randagravum chērttiṇakkām
'amma' yennappadamillā irunnenkilellām
nirarthamāyēne!

The two ends of the world can be joined with these two syllables. If the word "Amma" is not there, everything will become meaningless.

jīvalōkattin jayōtsavavēdiyil
kālamākunnēkasākṣi!

kālattinum sākṣiyākunna satyattin
kālkkal namikkān paṭhikkām

In the stage of celebrating the success of life, time is the only witness. Let us prostrate at the feet of that truth who is the witness even of time.

AMBE MAYAMAULI (MARATHI)

ambē māyamaulī
vidyēchi tū karī gē sāvalī
hē śubhravastradhāriṇī
vīṇā madhuravādinī
vīṇā madhuravādini

O Mother, my Mother, may I attain knowledge under Your divine guidance. O Goddess attired in pure white raiment, who plays the veena melodiously.

vāgadīśvari namō namaḥ
akhilāṇḍeśvari namō namah
śāradē tujhā namō namaḥ
jai jagadīśvari namō namaḥ

I bow down to the Goddess of speech, to the Goddess of all the worlds. My prostrations to Thou who art Mother Sharada, victory to the Goddess of the Universe!

ambē māyamaulī
subuddhīchī karī gē sāvalī
hē śōkamōhanāśinī
pāpabhītivibhañjinī
pāpabhītivibhañjini

O Mother, my Mother, help me develop a discriminative intellect. O Goddess who destroys sorrow, attachment, sins and fear.

ambē māyamaulī
vāngmayāchi karī gē sāvalī
hē bhaktalōkapālinī
prēma bhakti sandāyinī
prēma bhakti sandāyinī

O Mother, my Mother, help me develop depth in my words. O Goddess who looks after the world of devotees and bestows supreme devotion

ambē māyamaulī
ādyātmāchi karī gē sāvalī
hē hamsamandagāminī
jñāna mukti vidhāyinī
jñāna mukti vidhāyinī

O Mother, my Mother, help me develop spiritually, O Goddess whose graceful gait resembles that of a swan and who bestows knowledge and liberation.

AMBE GĀLANU (KANNADA)

ambe gālanu ikutta todala mātanu nuṭiyuva
attukareyuva kūsunānu kāppāṭammā

Mother, I am only a child. My steps are faltering and my speech is meaningless. I cry out to You; please take care of me.

ninna kōmalasparśavu santōṣa nandittu
jampu daniya tampali santāpa nīgittu

Your tender touch brings me immense joy. In the coolness of Your sweet voice my sorrows vanish.

ninna maṭilē amma entu nanagāsarē
jāribīladē iralu ammā avachikō kūsa
manadatumba tumbiha holasanellava nīgubā
prēmagangeya harisu ammā manava tumbikō

My dear Mother, Your lap is my only refuge. Please hold me tight so that I will never slip away. Shower Your love upon me to wash away the dirt in my mind. Let my heart become filled with You.

ninna mahimeya ariyuvā śaktiyēnu illavammā
belakachelli dhāritōru ammā nīnu
kaiya hiḍidu munnaṭesu ammā nanna
prēmabhakutiya varava nīḍu dayapālisu

Mother, I don't have the strength to understand Your divinity. Kindly shed light on the path that leads me to You. Hold my hands in Yours and bestow on me pure devotion to You.

AMĒ MĀ MAIYĀ (GUJARATI)

amē mā maiyā, tārā tē chaiyā
śaraṇē tārī āvyā mā
lai jā śo jō nayyā pār karāvjō
chōḍśō nahi madh dariyā mā

Mother, we Your little children have come under Your shelter. Please take this boat across (the ocean of birth and death). Don't abandon us in mid-stream!

raḍtā kakkaḍṭā paḍtā akhḍtā
dvārē tārī pahōnchyā mā
khōḷāmā lēśō hṛdayē lagāvśō
vāḷśō nahi pāchā sansār mā

Crying and weeping, falling and stumbling, we have reached Your door. Take us in Your lap, hold us close to Your heart. Please Mother, don't send us back to the world!

dvārē mā tārē kōḍiyā āvē
āvē dīn duḥkhiyā mā
duḥkhiyāna duḥkh harō
kōḍiyā na rog harō
āpī kanchan kāyā mā

At Your doorstep lepers come, the poor and sorrowful ones come. You remove the sorrows and take away the disease of the lepers, giving them a crystal clear skin.

chōḍśō nahi madh dariyā mā

O Mother, please don't abandon us in mid-stream!

AMMĀ AMMĀ ENA UNNAI (TAMIL)

ammā ammā ena unnai
anbuḍan azhaikkum ennai
ēreḍuttum pārātinnum
ēninta viḷayāṭṭammā

Why this play of Yours, Mother, of not sparing me a single glance when I call out to You with love, calling 'Mother, Mother'?

ēṇkiḍum en nilayaikkaṇḍu
uḷḷam innum iraṇkātat ēn
kanṭru nāḍi vantiṭum pōtu
kaniyāta tāyum uṇḍō

Why doesn't Your heart melt seeing my pitiable condition? Does the mother cow refuse to show mercy to the calf who comes searching for her?

anaittayumē aripavaḷanḍrō
entan uḷḷam ariyātavaḷo
tavaru enna seytēn ammā
tavarāmal ninaivāy ennai

You are all-knowing; can't You read my mind? Mother, what wrong did I commit? Keep me in Your thoughts for ever.

sērttu vaitta vinaikaḷai ellām
sērttukkoḷvāy un tāḷkaḷilē
pārttiḍammā kaḍaikkaṇ tirantu
iruvinaikaḷ muttrum nīṅka

Please accept all my accumulated sins at Your feet. Kindly cast Your divine glance to erase all my past misdeeds.

AMMĀ AMMĀ KŌṆĀCHĪ (KONKANI)

ammā ammā kōṇāchī
ammā sagalyā jagāchī
ammā amgele burgyāchī mōgāchī
mōgāchī mōgāchī amma mōgāchī mōgāchī

Who are Mother's children? She is the Mother of the entire universe. She is the darling Mother of all of Her children.

hāsatta amkā gēttāttī
khuśitta amkā soyittāttī
bhaktī amkā dīttāttī mōgāchī
mōgāchī mōgāchī amma mōgāchī mōgāchī

Mother welcomes us with love and watches over us with a smile. She is our own darling Mother who bestows devotion upon us.

manāka śānti dīttāttī
rekṣā amgele karttāttī
sukhātta amkā dvarttāttī mōgāchī
mōgāchī mōgāchī amma mōgāchī mōgāchī

One's mind finds peace when it rests in Mother. She takes care of us and makes sure that we are secure and safe.

AMMĀ NĀNUM (TAMIL)

ammā nānum nānāyirāmal
nīyāka mārūvatum eppozhutu
en uḷḷē nān senḍru
eṇṇankaḷaitu tān venḍru
nīyāka mārūvatum eppozhutu

Mother! When will I become You, leaving my identity behind? Going within, conquering all thoughts, when will I become one with You?

en sollum en sollāyirāmal
un sollāy mārūvatum eppozhutu
ammā ammā ammā ammā

Mother, when will my words, being no longer mine, become Yours?

en seyalē en seyalāy ākāmal
un seyalāy mārūvatum eppozhutu
ammā ammā ammā ammā

When will my actions, being no longer my own, become only Yours? O Mother, Mother.

en icchai en icchai ākāmal
un icchai ākūvatum eppozhutu
ammā ammā ammā ammā

When will my desires, being no longer my own, become Yours?

nanḍrum tītum mārinḍumē
enṭrum inbam sērndiḍumē
kāṇum kāṭcikaḷ yāvayumē
undan mayamāy māriḍumē

Good and bad may come and go, but happiness will always prevail. Your presence will prevail in all that is visible.

annāḷ varuvatum eppozhutu
nannāḷ varuvatum eppozhutu

When will that day come? When will that blessed day come?

AMMA NI SIRIKKAYILE (TAMIL)

amma ni sirikkayile
aṇḍamellām sirikkutammā
atai pārtta uyirkaḷellām
ānandattil sirikkutammā

Mother, when You smile, the whole universe smiles- seeing that all of creation laughs in ecstasy.

idayamatum sirikkutammā
idazh virittu sirikkutammā
puṇcirippai kaṇḍonṭrum
puriyāmal sirikkutammā

When it sees Your smile, the heart breaks into a smile, though it doesn't understand what it is all about.

kaivaḷaikaḷ sirikkutammā
kārcilambum sirikkutammā
mey uṇartti sirikkutammā
mēnmai kuṛi sirikkutammā

The bangles smile, the anklets smile. Everything smiles, forgetting itself, and praising Your greatness.

pūraṇamām un sirippil
puvi malarntu sirikkutammā
kāraṇankaḷ kāriyankaḷ
kaṭantu manam kaḷikkutammā

In Your smile, the world smiles, forgetting logic and activities.

AMMĀ UNTAN (TAMIL)

ammā untan kaivaḷayāy ākamāṭṭēnā
salankai kulunki naṭakkayilē pāṭamāṭṭēnā

Mother, make me Your bangle, so I may sing to the tune of Your jingling anklets as You walk!

ammā untan meṭṭi oliyāy māramāṭṭēnā
mēnmaimiku pādamtanai pattramāṭṭēnā
ammā

Mother, make me Your jingling toe ring, that I may dance with Your sacred feet!

ammā aṇiyum malaraṇiyāy māramāṭṭēnā
nintiruvaṭiyil malaritazhāy māramāṭṭēnā
ammā

Mother, make me the garland of flowers that adorns You, transform me into the petals that decorate Your lotus feet!

anudinamum un arukē irukkamāṭṭēnā
aḷavillā un anpil kaḷikkamāṭṭēnā
ammā

Mother, keep me near You every day and always, rejoicing in Your immeasurable love.

ammā un amudanāmam tutikkamāṭṭēnā
iṇaiyillā un ezhilil mūzhkamāṭṭēnā ammā

Mother, make me constantly chant Your nectarine name, immersed in Your incomparable beauty.

AMMANA DIVYA PĀDĀMBUJAGAḶIGE

(KANNADA)

ammana divya pādāmbujagaḷige
śirabāgu śirabāgu śirabāgu manujā
śirabāgu śirabāgu śirabāgu manujā

O Man, bow down to Mother's divine lotus feet.

māteya mamateya kṛpenamagādare
harivudu bhavabhaya chinteyatu
amṛtādēviya naukeyu doretare
bhavasāgarava dāṭuvevu

Mother's compassionate grace makes all our worries and fears disappear. Sailing on the Divine Mother's ship, we will cross the ocean of transmigration.

ella dharmagaḷa tiruḷanu sāruva
nondajīvige bharavase nīḍuva
ammana jīvana charitayanu
sāgaradalegaḷu sārutive

The very waves of the ocean declare that Mother's life story reveals the essence of all religions, and gives hope to suffering souls.

jagadambe śaraṇam jagadambe śaraṇam
jagadambe śaraṇam jagadambe śaraṇam

We seek refuge in You, O Mother of the Universe!

AMMANA NĀḌADU (TULU)

ammana nāḍadu bulpinā onji
bālēnātulē bālēnātulē
āṇḍa īrenā maḍilaḍa bālē āda jappōḍe
amma yāna jappoḍe

This child cries with longing for Mother, but can I sleep in Your lap like a baby, can I sleep?

bandhu panpina janakulu kai buḍudu pōvvēra
oṭṭige battinā dēvere kāppule
amma kāppule enklēnu amma kāppule

The people whom we call relatives will leave us and go. You are the divine one who is always with me. Protect me Mother! Take care of me, Mother, take care of me!

dhyāna eṇchina rūpa eṇchina enk gottiji

amma paṇḍudu buḷppēra mātra
enk barppuṇṭu amma enk barppuṇṭu

I know neither meditation nor form. I only know to cry, calling for Mother. That is all I know, Mother, that is all I know!

bhakti eṇchina mukti eṇchina enk gottiji
āṇṭa īṛanā pādakke śaraṇa
sādi tōjāle amma sādi tōjāle

I know neither devotion nor liberation; show me how to take refuge at Your feet! Please show me the way, Mother, please show me the way!

AMMAYALLE ENDAMMAYALLE

(TELUGU)

ammavēlē mā ammavēlē
kaṇṇīru tuḍicchē mā ammavēlē

Aren't Thou my Mother, O aren't Thou my dear Mother who wipes away the tears?

lōkālanēlē ammavēlē
ī viśvakāriṇi ammavēlē
ennāḷugānē pilicchēnu ninnē
śaktisvarupiṇi rāvēlanē

Aren't Thou the Mother of the 14 worlds, the Creatress of the world? Since how many days I am calling Thee, O Thou whose nature Shakti (energy). Won't Thou come?

sṛṣṭi shtitilaya samhāramantayu
iṣṭadānapriya nīlōnē lē
ennāḷugānē pilicchēnu ninnē
śakti svarupiṇāvēlanē

O Thou who loves to give the desired things, are not Creation, Preservation and Destruction in Thee? Since how many days.

vēdamu śāstramu vēdāntavidyayū
ādi maddhyāntamu nīvēnulē
ennāḷugānē pilicchēnu ninnē
śaktisvarupiṇi rāvēlanē

Aren't the Vedas, Scriptures, Knowledge of Vedanta, the beginning, middle and end all in Thee? Since how many days.

ĀNANDADHĀMAMĀM NINNILETTĀN

(MALAYALAM)

ānandadhāmamām ninnilettān
ātankitāntam kodicchidunnu
kaiyetthā durattāy nilppadendē ammē
kaivalyasāra swarupini ni

My sorrowful heart is yearning to reach You –the abode of bliss. Oh, essence of liberation! Why do You stand just out of reach?

vēdanayil tān tudangi janmam
vēdanayil tān oḍungiḍumō?
jīvanīr tēḍumī āturane
jagajīvanī nīyum maraniḍumō?

My birth had begun in pain. Will it also end in pain? Will the Mother of the Universe forget this sorrowful one who is in search of life?

sargattināmukhamānatennum
naisargika nombarmākayālō

jīvitam bhūvitil nishkarunam
īvidham yāthanā nirbharitam

Is life in this world mercilessly painful because of the pain in the preface of creation?

āmoda sāmrajya rānjniyām nin
āromalām putramānu ñānum
enkilum Ammē ennikkulatām
pankayi nī tanu ī shokarājyam

I am the son of the Empress of the domain of Bliss. Yet I inherit as my share this sorrowful world.

pinchilam paitalin punchiri pōl
peyavē nī chitta nairmalyamāy
nenjil ninnakay viringiḍunnu
mañilam pūvukal niramālaymāy

You shower purity in my heart like the smile of an infant. My heart blossoms dew-drop flowers in a beautiful garland.

ĀNANDAM ĀNANDAM ĀNANDAMĒ

(TAMIL)

ānandam ānandam ānandamē
paramānandam ānandam ānandamē

It is bliss, bliss, bliss! It is supreme bliss!

ammāvin kaḍaikkaṇ nammaiyum kaṇḍāl
ānandam ānandam ānandamē
avaḷ kaṇkaḷai imaittu punnakai purindāl
ānandam ānandam ānandamē

When Mother's glance falls on us, it is bliss. When She winks and smiles at us, it is bliss!

kaṭṭiyaṇaittu darisanam aḷittāl
ānandam ānandam ānandamē
nam kannattilē avaḷ muttam koṭuttāl
ānandam ānandam ānandamē

When She embraces us and gives us darshan, it is bliss. When She kisses our cheeks, it is bliss!

āṇandam ānandam ānandamē

It is bliss, bliss, bliss.

ammāvin sundara vadanam kaṇḍāl -
ānandam āṇandam ānandamē
alai kaḍalena puraḷum kūndalai kaṇḍāl -
ānandam ānandam ānandamē

It is bliss to see Mother's beautiful form; Her hair flows like the waves of the ocean.

sivamām sandanappōṭṭinai kaṇḍāl
ānandam ānandam ānandamē
atil saktiyāmkunkamam sērntiḍumpōḍ -
ānandam ānandam ānandamē

It is bliss to see sandal paste on Her forehead, representing Lord Shiva. When it is accompanied with kumkum (vermilion) representing Shakti, it is bliss!

ānandam ānandam ānandamē

It is bliss, bliss, bliss.

ĀNANDAMĒ ĀNANDAM (TAMIL)

ānandamē ānandam ennē enadu ānandam
anubhavamē anubhavam bhakti tanda anubhavam

O bliss, bliss! Intense is my bliss! O experience, experience! The experience that devotion gives me!

kaṇkaḷ raṇḍum kaṇṇanadu divyarūpam kāṇudē
kādiraṇḍum kāṇṇanadu venkuzhalil mayankudē
kaigaḷ raṇḍum kaṇṇankku veṇṇeyinai ūṭṭudē
kāliraṇḍum kaṇṇanoḍu āṭi āṭi kaḷikkudē

I behold Krishna's form with my two eyes. I become intoxicated hearing Krishna's flute with my two ears. I feed butter to Krishna with my two hands. I dance with Krishna with my two feet!

nāvumavan mīdivaitta avalin suvaiyai rusikkudē
nāsiyavan vanamālai narumaṇattai rasikkudē
vāyumavan līlaigaḷai pāṭippāṭi magizhudē
mēniyavan tīṇḍalilē mellatannai izhakkudē

The taste of the puffed rice He has eaten is on my tongue. I inhale the sweet fragrance of His garland of wild flowers. With my lips, I blissfully sing about His leelas. My body slowly merges into His form.

nirmalamām idayamavan kōyilāga ānadē
nittiyamum isaimalarāl pūjaitanai ceyyudē
arivumavan gītaiyenum amudattinai parugudē
āṇavamum avanaṭiyil sevaganāy paṇiyudē

My heart is becoming pure; now it is His temple! In my daily worship of Him, songs are the flowers I offer at His feet. My mind drinks the nectar of the Gita, and my ego falls at His feet. I am His servant.

ANBENUṀ SOLLUKKU AMMĀ (TAMIL)

anbenuṁ sollukku ammā - undan
anbinḍri nāṅkaḷiṅkillayē ammā
emaikākka ōtōṭi varuvāy - eṅkaḷ
idayattil enṭrenṭruṁ nī vīttriruppāy

Where would we be without You? You are pure love, Mother, come running to protect us and dwell in our hearts for ever!

annaiyāy vandavōr śakti - adu
akhilattirkkellāṁ vazhaṅkiṭuṁ mukti
ariyāmai akattriṭa vārāy - emmuḷ
aravāzhvu malarndiṭa un aruḷ tārāy

The power You possess as a mother brings salvation to the entire universe; kindly come to remove our ignorance and bless us with rightful living!

tuyar tīra nī tānē marundu - bhaktar
tūymaiyām manatirkku aruṁ peruṁ virundu
kavalaikaḷ nīkkiṭu tāyē - nāṅkaḷ
kaikūppi nittamuṁ vaṇaṅkiṭuvōmē

You are the cure for our sorrow. The purity of the seeker is the mind's real wealth. Please remove our worries, Mother, as we bow down before You with hands joined in prayer!

ANBU VAṬIVĀNAVAḶ (TAMIL)

jhala jhala
anbu vaṭivānavaḷ annaiyavaḷ varukirāḷ
akilattil vizhākkōlam annai makkaḷin porkkālam
amudamazhayāy avaniyil ānandamē pozhiya
ādiśakti bhuvanattil bavani varukirāḷ

That embodiment of love, the divine Mother, is coming! It is a universal festival, the Golden age for the children of the divine Mother. The Goddess of supreme power is coming, leading a procession to shower the nectar of bliss over the entire universe.

jhala jhalavena salankai kulunka
kalakalavena sirittukkoṇḍu
palapalapala līlai purintu bavani varukirāḷ
amma bavani varukirāḷ

Mother is leading the procession, anklets jingling. She is laughing, and performing many, many leelas!

om śakti parāśakti om śakti mahāśakti
akilattai aravaṇaittiṭa bavani varukirāḷ
ammā bavani varukirāḷ

The essence of Om, the ultimate power of the universe, is coming in a procession to embrace the world!

kāḷī mahākāḷī dēvī parāśaktī

Divine mother Kali, supreme power of the universe!

arttamillā vārttaikaḷai arttamuḷḷatākkivaittu
arttamillā siruvāzhvil anpatanai tantarūḷi
arttamuṭanē vāzhavaippāḷ anbunāyakī
akilalōka rakṣakiye jagadīśvarī

Filling empty words with significance, blessing our short, aimless lives with love, the Goddess of love, protector of all the worlds, the queen of the universe, will make our lives meaningful.

dēhamēgam sūzhntālum ātmasūrya oḷivīśum
ēkaśakti katiravanām parāśaktiyē
katiravanai tilakamākki tarittukkoṇḍavaḷē
kātaṇiyai veṇṇilāvāy māttri vaittavaḷē

Although we are surrounded by the dark clouds of body-consciousness, You come as the sun that showers us with the rays of consciousness. O Mother! You wore the sun as the tilakam mark on Your forehead and made Your earrings shine like the moon.

manamenum pū malarkiratu tēnenum bakti niraikiratu
manakōvilil niraintiṭa dēvī varukirāḷ
kaliyukattin iruḷ maraya aruḷ vēṇḍumē
kalidōṣam nīkka jñāna mazhai vēṇḍumē

The flower of the mind opens, and is filled with the honey of devotion. Devi is coming to reside in the temple of the mind. We need Her grace to remove the darkness of Kali Yuga. We need the divine shower of self knowledge to remove the evils of Kali Yuga.

ANGUM INGUM (TAMIL)

angum ingum alaindiṭṭāy
amaidi tēḍi kaḷaittiṭṭāy
adu undan manattirukka
arindiḍāmal ēn alaindāy

You are exhausting yourself, roaming here and there in search of peace. Peace is within you, but unaware of this, you wander.

iruppiḍattai māttri viṭṭāy
enḍrālum amaidi uṇḍō
viruppamellām niraivu seytāy
vēṇḍiyadu kiṭaittaduṇḍō

You tried moving from place to place, yet have not found peace. You have tried to satisfy all your desires; have you found what you were searching for?

param poruḷin padam paṇivāy
parivuḍanē vazhi naṭattum
sadguruvai caraṇaḍaivāy
śāntiyadum tānēvarum

Prostrate at the feet of the Supreme, and compassionately you will be led. Surrender to the sadguru, and peace will come to you on its own.

ANNAI ENṬRA SONDAMĀ (TAMIL)

annai enṭra sondamā
anbu koḷḷuṁ bandamā
karuṇai uḷḷa neñchamē
kaninda bhakti aruḷumē

Is this a motherly relation? Or is it a bondage of love? Only a compassionate mind will bless us with deep devotion.

dharmmaṁ kākkuṁ tāyena
dharaṇi vanda durggayē
kattravar pōttriṭuṁ
karmam tīrkkuṁ annaiyē

O Mother Durga, You have come down onto this earth to be the protector of righteousness. The learned praise You, O Mother, You are the remover of our sins.

dīpaṁ kāṭṭuṁ chuṭarilē
dēvi mukhaṁ tōnṭrumē
pāpachumaikaḷ tīrndiṭa
pārvai onṭru pōtumē

Your divine countenance shines forth in the arathi flame. By Your glance alone, You remove the burden of our sins.

tēṭi vandōṁ sannidhi
dinamuṁ kiḍaikkuṁ nimmati
karpakaṁ nī allavā
kaikoṭuttu kākkavā

We are seeking Your presence to find everlasting peace. Are You not the celestial Karpagam tree, offering us Your protecting hand?

annaiyuṁ nīyē tātayuṁ nīyē
ādarittaruḷuṁ deyvamuṁ nīyē
annaiyuṁ nīyē tātayuṁ nīyē
ādarittaruḷuṁ deyvamuṁ nīyē

You are indeed our Mother and Father, and the God who is our saving grace.

ĀVI AMBA ĀVI AMBA (BANDALO IN GUJRATI)

āvi amba āvi amba
āvi amba āvi amba
āvi amba āvi ḥṛdayeśvari
kārunyarupini padhāri

lāl cundaddi odhine āvi
mand muskān karti
hāth banne pasāri kaheti
doddi āvo ballako badha
padhāri kārunyarupini padhāri

sahune haiye lagāvavā
haiyye lagāvi cumbana devā
ballakone āshish deva
āshish āpi var deva
padhāri kārunyarupini padhāri
kaṣta badhā dur karavā
nijānanda varsāvavā
agnāni aevā āpanane
ānandamā magna karvā
padhāri kārunyarupini padhāri

ĀYARKULA KOZHUNTE (TAMIL)

āyarkula kozhunte, kaṇṇā
adiyum antamum unniḍatte
vedamum otuvate, kaṇṇā
venkuzhal ōsaiyai en agatte

Oh Kanna, hope of the Yadava clan, time begins and ends in You. The music of Your flute, the essence of the Vedas, is within me.

un mukham kāṇavillai, kaṇṇā
uriyavan nī ennai seravillai
uṇṇavum viruppamillai, kaṇṇā,
urakkamum kaṇkaḷai tazhuvavillai
ennaiye piḍikkavillai, kaṇṇā
innilai nīḍittāl artthamillai

I cannot see Your face, Kanna. I belong to You, but You have not yet merged in me. I do not feel like eating, Kanna, nor does sleep caress my eyes. If this continues, if You don't care for me, Kanna, my life has no meaning.

munnamezh pirappinilum, kaṇṇā
unnaiye ninaindu urukiniṇḍren
ninnaiye saraṇaḍainten, kaṇṇā,
pinnaiye pirintoru vazhiyariyen
innamum tāmatamo, kaṇṇā
ennai izhantu karaintiḍuven

Oh Kanna, for the last seven births I have been melting in thoughts of You. I surrender to You, Kanna. Without You, I know no other way. So why do You delay, Kanna? When will I merge in You, letting go of my ego?

oṭivā cinnakaṇṇā
oru muttam tantiḍu cellakaṇṇā
āṭivā cinnakaṇṇā
anta ānandam tantiḍu cellakaṇṇā

Come running, little Kanna, darling Kanna, give me a kiss. Come dancing Kanna, grant me the bliss of Your vision, darling Kanna.

AZHIYĀDA ĀNANDAM (TAMIL)

azhiyāda ānandam taruvāḷ
annaiyiṭam aṭaikkalam aṭaintiṭuvōm
nilayillā ulakil iruntālum
nilaiyāna tuṇaiyāy irintiṭuvāḷ

Let us seek refuge in Mother: She will bestow eternal bliss. Even though we live in an impermanent world, She guides us as our constant companion.

vazhikāṭṭa nīyum maruttuviṭṭāl
vazhimāri pōyviṭuvōm tāyē
takuti illāmmal iruntālum
un tāḷkaḷ nāḍiyē vantēnē

Mother, if You refuse to show us the path to God, we will be lost. Even though we are unfit for Your grace, still we come, seeking refuge at Your feet.

gati vēṇḍum ēnkiṭum un sēyai
vidhi vēṇḍum vazhi senṭru vīzhāmal
ati vēgam un aruḷāsiyināl
matimayakkam nīkki unnaṭi sērppāy

O Mother, this child has come seeking refuge. Please don't send me away on the path destined by my fate. Please bless this child quickly with Your grace, lift the veil of dizzying Maya and grant me refuge at Your feet!

BĀ BĀRŌ MANAVE BHAJISU NĪ HARIYA (KANNADA)

bā bārō manave bhajisu nī hariya
bā bārō manave bhajisu nī hariya
bā bārō manave bhajisu nī hariya

O Mind, come and worship Hari

alediruve ellī yārā huḍukutihe allilli
kaṇḍu kāṇisade nā aḍagiruve ninnalli
āgasavāgalu nīnu hṛdayapuṣpa varaḷuvudu
sugandhava nīnāga ariyuve – ō manavē
bā bārō manave bhajisu nī hariya

Where are you roaming? What are you searching for here and there? Can you not see that I am within you? Become as expansive as space, your heart will blossom like a flower, and you will then experience its fragrance. O Mind, come and worship Hari.

dāhavinnu tīradu nōḍu marubhūmi idayyā
śītala nīrilla bari kanasu mātravayyā
maraḷi hōgalu ninnoḷage kuḷitu nī dhyānadi
kāṇisuve nānāga beḷakāgi – ō manave
bā bārō manave bhajisu nī hariya

This is a desert, your thirst cannot be quenched here; in truth there is no water, it is but a dream. Sit in meditation, return to your Real Self – I will then appear in the form of light! O Mind, come and worship Hari.

marugadiru yārilla ninna jotegendu tiḷidu
hariyu iralu jotage śakutiyanu biḍadiru
narajanumava paḍedāga bērēnu bēku ninage

saṅkaṭa biḍu bā bēgā ōḍōḍi – ō manave
bā bārō manave bhajisu nī hariya

Don't be mournful, thinking that no one is with you. Don't give up, the Lord is at your side! Within this human life, what more is required? Leave all your sorrows behind and come running quickly! O Mind, come and worship Hari.

malagiruve yāke tiḷidu ellava nī summane
eddēḷu karmavāgisikō nijamantra
prēmabhakutiya tumbi japisutali naḍe munde
yāra hangēke ninage tumbiralu nā manadi
- bā bārō manave bhajisu nī hariya

Knowing all this, why are you still asleep? Wake up, let action be your true mantra, and move forward with love and devotion. Why depend on others when I am in your mind? O Mind, come and worship Hari.

BĀ BHṚNGAVĒ BĀ (KANNADA)

bā bhṛngavē bā
mana bhṛngavē bā
ammana karēyitu kēḷisadē?
ētakē aḷutiruvē?

Come, O honey-bee of the mind! Don't you hear Amma calling? Why are you crying?

hoḷeva dhavaḷa hṛdaya kamala
miḍididē prēma taranga
madhuva saviye savidu kuṇiye
makāra moḷaguta bā

The resplendent, white lotus of the heart throbs with vibrations of love. Come, chanting the divine syllable, 'Ma', so that you may taste the nectar and rejoice!

bēganē bantu madhuva uṇḍu
mēlakēruva bā
allidē ānanda allidē āmōda
amṛtapāna allidē bā

Come soon to drink the nectar, and then let us ascend. Come! There is real bliss, there is real joy. There is the real drink of immortality.

hē manabhṛnga! hē manabhṛnga!
hē manabhṛnga! hē manabhṛnga!

O honey-bee of the mind!

BAḌĪ DUVIDHA MĒ (HINDI)

baḍī duvidha mē hū bhagavan
tumi kai sē ārādhū mē
kōyī mādhyama nahī aisā
jisē pūjā mē lāūn mè

I am in great misery, O Lord. How am I to worship You? I know of no proper manner in which to worship You.

tumhārī jyōti sē jagamaga hē
ravi rajnīś aur tārē
mahā andhēra hōgā ra tumhē
dīp dikhāūn mai

It is Your effulgence that illumines the universe; it is You who shine through the sun, the moon and the stars. What terrible ignorance would it be for me to light a lamp before You?

tumhī hō phūl aur phala mē tumhī
basatē hō khuśhbū mē
bhalā bhagavān kō bhagavān par
kaisē chaḍhāūn mai

You give life to the fruits and flowers in this world and You give sweetness to their fragrance. How then can I offer You unto Yourself?

tumhī hō vyāpta jal tal mē
tumhī maujūd kaṇ kaṇ mē
anādar hai bulānē kō agar
ghanṭi bajāūn mai

You are in every drop of the great expanses of water. Would it not show disrespect to call You with a mere ringing of bells?

BANDAḶŌ BANDĀḶŌ (KANNADA)

bandaḷō bandāḷō amma
bandaḷō bandāḷō
bandaḷō bandāḷō hṛdayēśvarī
kāruṇyarūpadī bandāḷō

Here comes Mother, the Goddess of my heart, in the form of compassion!

paṭṭusīre dharisi bandāḷō
honnageya bīrutali
kaiyeraḍu bīsutali
ōṭi banni makkaḷe yentu karedāḷō
kāruṇyarūpadi bandālō

Decked in golden silk, beaming with golden smiles, swinging both of Her hands, calling "Come running, O children!" She comes in the form of compassion.

ellarannu tabbikkoḷḷalu
tabbikkoṇḍu muttanīḍalu
ellarannu anugrahisalu
anugrahisi varanīḍalu bandāḷō
kāruṇyarūpadī bandāḷō

She comes to embrace every one of us, to kiss every one of us, to bless us all and grant us our wishes. She comes in the form of compassion.

kaṣṭakaḷa pariharisalu
nijānanda tōrisalu
ajñānikaḷāda namannu
ānandadi muḷugisalu bandāḷō
kāruṇyarūpadī bandāḷō

She comes to solve our problems and to show us real bliss. She comes to drown us, ignorant ones, in bliss. She comes in the form of compassion.

BANDAMUṆṬU SONTAMUṆṬU

(TAMIL)

bandamuṇṭu sontamuṇṭu kaṇṭu koṇṭē nān ammā
enṭra zhaiku bōtu varum bandam nilaitān

I feel a bond as if with a relative, with someone I can call my own. I call out, "Amma," and then the connection is firmly established.

maṇam vīsum malar nukarntu
unnai ninaintēn manatil
ar chanaikal seytu nānum ennai marantēn
tēnum pālum abhiṣēkam seytu makizhtēn
anta kā chi kaṇṭa entan ullam pūrītti runtēn

When I see fragrant flowers I remember You and when I chant Your names I forget myself. I delight in worshipping You with honey and milk; the sight of such worship fills my heart.

tāyāki tantayumāy guruvum āna dēvi inke
nirguṇamāy tōnṭruvatai kaṇṭu viyantēn
vazhiyariyā pētayāy kaṇṇīrōṭu ninṭēn
anta śankari azhaika piravi payanai aṭaintēn

The Divine Mother is my mother, father and guru and yet She is also attributeless; Her mysterious nature is thus astonishing. This poor one does not know the true path and so I remain where I am with tear filled eyes. I call out, "Shankari," and then I feel the purpose of my birth.

ariyāmai irul sūr uzhanṭu nānum iruntēn
annai untan arulāl karuṇaikaṭalil matintēn
amgam amgam āka ennai arppaṇam seytēn
tāyē nī āla vēṇṭum dayavai kāttiruntēn

From the darkness of ignorance I have been immersed, by Your grace, in the sea of Your compassion. I offer all parts of myself to You; I wait for You to become firmly established as the ruler of my heart.

BANDU BIḌABĀRADĒ (KANNADA)

bandu biḍabāradē bāgilanu tērēdu ni
hṛdaya bāgilanu tērēdu ni
ariyalārenu nānu bāgilanu tērēyalu
hṛdaya bāgilanu tērēyalu

Why don't You come, and open the door Yourself, the door of the heart? I don't know how to open the door of my heart.

mareyutihēnu nāni manada māyeyalī ninna
endendu mareyada hāge
bandu ni nelesabāradē

Caught in the maya of the mind, I forget You. Why don't You come and settle in my heart so that I may never, ever forget You?

ammā ammā endu kareyutiruvēnu ninna
kāyutiruvēnu tāyē ninna baruvikege nānu

I call out to You, Amma, Amma! O Mother, I am waiting for You to come.

BĀRA GŌPĀLA BĀLĀ GŌPĀLABĀLĀ (KANNADA)

bāra gōpāla bālā gōpālabālā
he bāla gōpālabālā

Come, O little Gopala!

bēḷagāgi nāveddu yāryyāra neneyōṇā
bālana pādava nenayōṇā
bālakṛṣṇanā bangāra pādake
śirabāgi kaiyyā mugiyōṇā

As we rise in the morning, who shall we remember? We shall remember the feet of the little One. We shall bow to the golden feet of the little Krishna, with palms joined.

nandana nandana gōpikā chandana
vēṇuvilōlana neneyōṇā
beṇṇekaḷḷā śri yaśōda nandana
bhaktiyindā nāvu bhajisōṇā

Let us remember Nanda's son, the moon of Gopis, the One who plays on flute. Let us sing with devotion to the butter thief, who is Yashoda's son.

dēvaki putranā paṇḍava guruvana
rādhākṛṣṇana neneyoṇā
gītā nāthā śri kṛṣṇana neneyutta
koraletti hāḍi naliyōṇā

Let us remember Devaki's son, the Guru of Pandavas, who is Radhakrishna. Remembering Sri Krishna who is the Lord of Gita, let us sing joyfully.

navilina gariyanu śiradali muḍidiha
nīlaśarīrī gōpī kṛṣṇā
chittachōrā mana yamunāṭaṭadali
rāsalīle gende kādiddānē
bāra gōpāla bāla

The blue-bodied Gopikrishna is wearing the peacock feather in His head. The thief of my heart is waiting on the banks of Yamuna of my mind for the sake of playing rasalila.

BHAKTARU BANDIHARU (KANNADA)

bhaktaru bandiharu dēgulake
darśana nīḍu dēva śivane

We devotees have come to the temple. O Lord Shiva, grant us Your darshan!

nāgahāra darisiruve dēva
gangēya hottiruve śiva
candrana śiradali muḍidiruve dēva
bhasmava pūśiruve śiva

O Lord, Your neck is encircled by a snake-garland. O Shiva, You bear the river Ganga on Your head. You have adorned Your head with the crescent moon, and smeared sacred ash on Your body.

ōm namaḥ śivāya ōm namaḥ śivāya
kāḷakūṭa kuṭidavane dēva
kailāsa nāthane śiva
vighnēśa murugēśa tantayē dēva
pārvati priyakarane śiva

O Lord who has drunk the Kalakoota poison, O Shiva, Lord of Kailash; You are the father of Ganesh and Muruga, O Shiva, You are dear to Parvati.

kēḷannu morayannu dēva
kāruṇya mūrttiye śiva
gagana samudra hudugiruve dēva
ninagāgi kādiruve śiva

O Lord, embodiment of compassion, listen to my plea. I have crossed the sky and the sea in search of You; O Shiva, I have waited for You alone.

ānanda rūpane dēva
viśvaika nāthane śiva
paśupati nāthane praḷayāntakarane
praṇava svarūpane dēva amṛta lingave śiva

O Lord, embodiment of bliss, You stand as the only Lord of the Universe; O Shiva, Lord of animals, cause of dissolution, embodiment of the primordial sound Om, Your form is the immortal lingam.

BIRŌHER (BENGALI)

birōher āgūne jōlichē hṛdōy
bōlitē nārī tōre bidāy
mā hōye mōre bhulē gēlī
kālī tuḷa hōli mṛṇmōyi

How can I say goodbye to You, while my heart burns in the fire of separation? How could You, being the mother, forget me? Oh Kali, you are the Earth itself.

bhēbē dēkh mātuyi nije
jōgōt bhūle ēnu tōrkāchē
tōr nōyōne subi nijere bhūlē
tāu ki nibinā kōlē tulē?

O Mother, just see for Yourself. Abandoning the world, I have come to You. Forgetting myself, I surrender to Your gaze. Will You not take me into Your lap?

hāriye kōtō diḍēr mājeja
phāgōḷ hōlāmam tōke khuje
ār kōrō na dērī ō mā
lōkhi hōyē nāumā kōlē

Having lost myself running in so many directions, I have gone mad searching for You. Don't wait any longer, O Mother! Be kind to me, and take me into Your lap.

BĪT CALĀ (HINDI)

bīt calā mama ik aur janm

I have wasted one more lifetime.

man kē bandhan aur badhāyē
bhavan bharm kē hi nirmāyē
nācā jaysē nāc nacāyē
abhilāṣā mē māya sargam

The bondages of the mind have increased. My material desires are enslaving me, making my mind reel.

sat nahī jānā tat nahī jānā
param pitā kō nahī pehcānā
man kō nit ras naval pilāyē
pyāsā phir bhi rah gayā ātam

I have forgotten the real truth. I can't recognize my relationship with the Lord of lords. I am busy feeding my mind with new and enchanting desires of the senses, but my heart is still thirsty.

sab rūpōm mē tūhī samāyā
man andhiyārā dēkh na pāyā
jo khōjā mai antar tam mē
duśman pāyā apnā hī man

Although You are present in all forms, my ignorant mind cannot see You. When I searched for You within, my own mind became the adversary.

prabhū man kā andhiyārā miṭāō
dil mē nēhā kī jōt jalāvō
ab āyā hūṅ tērē dvārē
sah nahī pāvūṅ virhā kā gam

O Lord, please remove this darkness from my mind. Please light the lamp of devotion in my heart. I have come ignorant to Your door, and cannot bear this feeling of separation any longer. Please have mercy on me!

CĒNMILĒ (HINDI)

cēnmilē ārām milē
śānti ōr viśrām milē
vō he mā kigōd vimal
jahā bhaktōn kō prēm milē

Our sweet Mother's lap is so soft. Her devotees find quietude, peace, and unconditional love there.

snigdhasnēh apār mile
karuṇā aparampārmilē
vō hē mā kā hṛdayakamal
jahā hari ōmkār mile

Our sweet Mother's heart is like a lotus flower where Her devotees experience divine union and limitless compassion. In Her heart lord Hari resides and the divine sound Om resounds.

duḥkh dard santāp miṭē
ādhivyādhi abhiśāp miṭē
vō he mā kā hṛdaycaman
jahām kāṇṭō kā uttāp miṭē

Our sweet Mother's heart is like a beautiful garden. Her presence removes curses, pain and suffering. In Her lap, grief-stricken hearts find inner peace.

lōbh mōh sē trāṇ mile
kāmkrōdh kō virām mile
vō hē mā kā hṛdaygagan
jahā gangā kī dhār mile

In our divine Mother's heart flows the holy river Ganga. In Her lap devotees find freedom from greed and material attachments. Mother's presence purifies the hearts of Her darling children by bringing an end to lust and anger.

CĒSĒNU TALLI ABHIṢĒKAM (TELUGU)

cēsēnu talli abhiṣēkam
cērchave nannu āvali tīram

I worship You, Mother; take me to the other shore!

nī pādamudratō niṇḍina
suddhamaina manasuniyyamani
kōrutū cēsēnu abhiṣēkam
nī pādamulaku kṣirābhiṣēkam

Asking for a pure mind filled with the vision of Your feet, I worship Thy feet with milk.

nirantaram nī nāmajapamutō
manasu niścalamavvālani
kōrutū cēsēnu abhiṣēkam
nī pādamulaku dadhyābhiṣēkam

Seeking stillness of mind by constantly chanting Your holy name, I worship Thy feet with curd.

nā cintanalu ēkāgramai
nī diśalō pravahiñcālani
kōrutū cēsēnu abhiṣēkam

nī pādamulaku neyyabhiṣēkam

Wishing for concentration, and for my thought to flow towards You, I worship Thy feet with ghee.

nī madhurasmṛtulalō munigi
lōkamulō cēdu tākkoddani
kōrutū cēsēnu abhiṣēkam
nī pādamulaku tēnābhiṣēkam

To dwell in sweet memories of You, untouched by the negativity of the world, I worship Thy feet with honey.

nī prēmasvarūpamū
nā madilō sadā nilavālani
kōrutū cēsēnu abhiṣēkam
nī pādamulaku pannīrābhiṣēkam

Wishing for Your loving form to remain in my mind always, I worship Thy feet with perfumed water.

CHOLLU SAKHĪ (MALAYALAM)

chollu sakhī, nammal oru mātrayenkilum
ariyāte mizhiyaṭacchirunnu pōyō?
atunēram maṇivarṇṇan kaṭannu pōyō, namu—
kkorū nōkkū kāṇān iṭatarāte?

Tell me friend, did we unknowingly let our eyes close, for but a moment? And did darling Krishna get away, meanwhile, without giving us the chance for even a glimpse?

matiyō – mizhīyō – parayū sakhī, namme
chatipiṇayicchatu hatavidhiyō?
nizhalanakkangalum, ilayilakkangalum
ariyāte mizhiyaṭacchirunnu pōyō?

Tell me dear friend, what was it that betrayed us - was it our mind, our eyes, or our sad fate? Did we just sit there with eyes closed, unaware of the movement of shadows or fluttering of leaves?

nalamoṭi malarikal ariyasugandham
vitari vitarnnaṇiyaṇiyaṇiyāy
varavētta tāreyannārāyukil – sakhī
'vanamāli' yenōtum vanarājikal!

If we ask the forests the question 'Whom did the lovely flowers welcome, lining up and spreading such beautiful fragrance?', the forests will answer, 'Vanamali' (He who is adorned with a garland of wild flowers)!

orutundu mayilpīlī kaḷaññukitti – kāttil
parannu vannariyāten matiyil vīṇu!
ezhunnelkkamal sakhī! kaṇṇan varunnatin
sandeśamāṇu – nām dhanyaratre!

I have found a fragment of peacock feather – it came flying in the wind and fell in my lap! Let us get up, my friend! This is a message that Krishna is coming. We are indeed blessed!

CITTACŌRANA (KANNADA)

cittacōrana kṛṣṇā mukundanā
bhajisuvā mōdadī ānanda kandanā

Let us delight in worshipping Krishna, Mukunda, the blissful child who has captured our hearts.

navajala dharasama nīlanā
murahara madhumaya rūpanā
agha hara karuṇā lōlanā
kaivalya dāyaka kṛṣṇanā

Let us delight in worshipping Krishna! Blue-hued and beautiful, He is the remover of sins, the destroyer of the demon Mura. He is compassionate, and He will grant us ultimate liberation.

agaṇita guṇamaya dēvanā
cyutiyē illada acyutanā
ghana karuṇāḷu kēśavanā
muraḷīdhara mucukundanā

Let us delight in worshipping Muchukunda, the lord with infinite attributes, the flawless One, Keshava, who holds the flute and is full of compassion.

CŌLTĒ CŌLTĒ (BENGALI)

cōltē cōltē dinēr śēśē
pōth hāriyē ekōn mōṭē
dāḍiyē āchi ōndhōkārē
ki hōbhē ōtīt bēbhē

Walking alone at the end of the day, you have lost your way and stand in the dark at the crossroads. What use is thinking of the past now?

kī pābi tui ētō khūnjē
nēykē kichū pābhār mōtōn
jā āchē tāō hariyē jābē
thākbhē nākō kichu hātē

What will you find after all your searching? Nothing is worth acquiring; whatever you have will also be lost. In the end, nothing will remain.

jānbi kōbē dēkhiś bhēbē
dēhēr prōti māyā kēnō
bhujtē hōlē egōtē hōbhē
jētē hōbē mōn pēriyē

Think about it. When will you finally understand? Why so much attachment to the body? To realize the truth, you need to move forward, and go beyond the mind.

lāgē bhōy jōdi mōnē
dēkhē niś tuyi pīchōn pānē
śāthē āchē kālō mēyē
egiyē jā tār nām niyē

If you feel frightened, just turn around. Look! The dark-hued One is with you. Keep on chanting Her name.

CUTTUNIRI (TAMIL)

vendaṇalāy tavittiṭum en manam
āriṭa siridanbai pozhintiṭu
untan aṭiyārin aṭiyārkkaṭiyanām
entan tuyarinai yāriṭam kūruvēn

tūya bhaktiyām nalvaram vēṇḍiyē
nīṇḍa nāṭkaḷāy unnai paṇikirēn
anbarukkaruḷ tandiṭum ambikē
untan karankaḷāl toṭṭaruḷ śeyguvāy

kūttruvan vandu kūppiṭum vēḷaiyil
kūṭṭaiviṭṭu parandiṭum ennuyir
śērttu vaittadum śērkka ninaittadum
kūṭa vandiṭātenbadum uṇmayē

ennai ēn inda kārirūḷ tannilē
vanmayāgattēḷḷi vadhaikkirāy
uḷḷattunbakkaṭal nīnkavē dinam
un aruṭpārvai ennil patittiṭu

uravu śolliṭa yāruḷar annayē
unnaiyanṭri i vaiyattil enṭrumē
ninnaiyē śārndu nirkkum nal uḷḷamum
innum tunbachumai ēndi nirppatō

samsārakkaṭal tanni lē manam
sadā mūzhgittavikkudē mahēśvari
tunba kaṭalai kaṭandu karai sēra
tāyē nin pāda ninaivai taruga nī

ḌAM ḌAM ḌUM ḌUM ḌAMARŪ BŌLE

(GUJARATI)

ḍam ḍam ḍum ḍum ḍamarū bōle
har har har har mahādevā
śiv śiv śiv śiv śivagaṇa bōle
namaḥ śivāya ōm namaḥ śivāya

The damaru is chanting 'har har har har mahadeva'- in response the Shiva Ganas are chanting 'namah shivaya.'

nīla nīla ākāś bōle
har har har har mahādevā
garjjanā kartā mēgh bōle
namaḥ śivāya ōm namaḥ śivāya

The blue sky chants 'har har har har mahadeva'. In response, the blue clouds roar 'namah shivaya om namah shivaya'.

sāgar nadī sarītā bōle
har har har har mahādevā
ghāṭ ghāṭ ne kinārā bōle
namaḥ śivāya ōm namaḥ śivāya

The oceans, the rivers and streams chant 'har har har har mahadeva,' and all the coasts and banks chant 'namah shivaya om namah shivaya' in response.

dhartti van parvat bōle
har har har har mahādevā
vṛkṣa latā ne śikharo bōle
namaḥ śivāya ōm namaḥ śivāya

The earth, the forests and the mountains chant 'har har har har mahadeva'. The trees, the creepers and the mountain tops chant 'namah shivaya om namah shivaya' in response.

ḍāḷ ḍāḷ par pankhī bōle
har har har har mahādevā
nṛttya karantā mōr bōle
namaḥ śivāya ōm namaḥ śivāya

The birds on every branch chant 'har har har har mahadeva'. In response, the peacocks dance, chanting 'namah shivaya om namah shivaya'.

vāṇi vidyā vādya bōle
har har har har mahādevā
sūr sangīt ne sār bōle
namaḥ śivāya ōm namaḥ śivāya

Speech, knowledge and musical instruments chant 'har har har har mahadeva'. All of music, every tune, and every essence chants 'namah shivaya om namah shivaya' in response.

sādhu sant bairāgi bōle
har har har har mahādevā
tum ham sab milkar bōle
namaḥ śivāya ōm namaḥ śivāya

The sages, the saints and the renunciates chant 'har har har har mahadeva'. Let us all chant 'namah shivaya om namah shivaya' in response!

DĀO DĀO DĀO MŌRE (BENGALI)

dāo dāo dāo mōre bhokti dāo mā
bhokti dāo prema dāo biśśāś dāo
bhokti dāo prema dāo biśśāś dāo
antahin srișți mā jhe māyyārī kelā
tōmārī kela șettō tōmārī līlā

Mother, please give me devotion. Give me devotion, divine love, and faith. This endless creation is a play by maya (illusion), it is nothing other than Your play, Your divine play.

jīboner potte jāttō badhā āśukk mā
pāy nābhōy pāy nābhōy pāy nābhōy
tumī ācch sāth mā tōbe kāre bhōy
hobe jōy hobe jōy hobe jōy

I will not be troubled by any of the obstacles that arise along the walk of life. Mother, with You by my side, who is there to fear? Victory will be with me!

kōyilāśō bhāśinī tumī singhobāhini
śaśono bhāśinī tumī muṇḍamālinī
bindubhāśinī tumī tripurēśśorī
jagōdīśśorī tumī śarbēśorī

You are Kailasavasini (She who dwells in Mount Kailash), and Simhavahini (She who rides upon a lion). You are Smasanavasini (She who dwells in the cremation grounds) and Mundamalini (She who bears a garland of human skulls). You are Binduvasini (She who resides in the center) and Tripureswari (Goddess of the three cities). You are Jagadiswari (Goddess of the Universe) and Sarveswari (Goddess of all).

DĀŚARATHĒ RAGHU (KANNADA)

dāśarathē raghurāmana nenedare ī
bhavasāgara dāṭṭuvudū
dōṣarahita śrīrāmana nenedare
cira sukha sampada dorakuvudū

The remembrance of Dasaratha's son, Raghurama, will carry us over this ocean of transmigration. When we think of the righteousness of Sri Rama, we are overwhelmed with happiness.

daśaratha nandana dānava bhaṇjana
daśaśira hāraṇa śrīrāma
paśupati mitrana pāpavimōcana
atiśaya dindali nene manavē

O mind, think fondly of Sri Rama, Dasaratha's son, the destroyer of demons, the killer of ten-headed Ravana, the friend of Lord Shiva, and the remover of all sins.

kauśika yāgava kāyita śrīrāmana
haruṣadindali nī nenemanavē
paramapāvana sītārāmana
nenedare durita duhkha tolaguvudū

O mind, remember Sri Rama joyfully! With the memory of the most auspicious Sitarama all your troubles and sorrows will fly away.

jṇānabhakti vairāgyava nittu
prēmadi poreyō śrīrāma
jōḍisi karagaḷa bēṭidare anudina
kāyvanu bhaktara śrīrāma

O Sri Rama, lovingly protect us by granting us knowledge, devotion and dispassion. If we pray to Lord Rama every day with folded hands, He will protect us and all His devotees.

DAYAKARŌ TUM (HINDI)

dayakarō tum gaṇēśa hamkō
nihārō karunā sē
subuddhi de dō vipatti harlō
tumī sahārā hō

O Lord Ganesh, have mercy on us. Please look upon us with compassion. O Lord, grant us supreme wisdom and remove our miseries

jay jay jay gaṇēśa jay gaṇēśa jay jay
jay gaṇēśa jay gaṇēśa jay jay
jay gaṇēśa jay gaṇēśa jay jay jay

Victory to Lord Ganesh!

gaṇēśa vardō gajāsya vardō
vardō vighnaharā
tumārī karunā hamārē ūpar
sadā banī rahē

O Ganesh, You are the remover of all obstacles. Please bless us and fulfill our desires. May Your grace and compassion be ever upon us!

girindranandini suputrahō tum
bhaktōm kē vardātā
mahēśanandana tumē hamārā
praṇām hē dēvā

You are the son of the daughter of the Lord of the mountains (Parvati), You bestow boons on all devotees. Our salutations to You, O son of Lord Shiva.

DAYAGALA MĀ AMMĀ (TELUGU)

dayagala mā ammā
nanu maruvakammā
nannuviḍici peṭṭaka
tīsukupō nīvenṭa
ānandalōkāllē cūpincagā

Oh my benevolent Mother! Please don't forget me. Don't abandon me. Take me with you to the world of divine bliss!

ī mūla āmalupu
dāranatā telusu
āpadalanu tappistu
tīsukupō nīvenṭa
ānandalōkāllē cūpincagā

Show me the way, take me along each twist and turn of life, avoiding every pitfall and danger. Take me with you to the world of divine bliss!

āṭṭabommala mōjulō
nī cēyī vadilēnēcō
nīvē nā cēyī paṭṭuku
tīsukupō nīvenṭa
ānandalōkāllē cūpincagā

Distracted by worldly objects, I might let go of your hand. So, hold on to my hand, and take me with You to the world of divine bliss!

lōtū pātulakū bediri
nē nilici na
pasidānni bharinci
tīsukupō nīvenṭa
ānandalōkāllē cūpincagā

If I stand still, afraid of the ups and downs of life, please bear with me, Your little child, and take me with You to the world of divine bliss!

DĒHACHYĀ MŪRALĪTA GĪTĒCHĀ VĀRĀ (MARATHI)

dēhachyā mūralīta gītēchā vārā
karmachyā vīnēlā bhaktīchā tārā

The flute in the form of a body is played by the wind of the Gita. A vina of karma having the strings of devotion.

karū prabhuchē kāma
rē mājhā mūkhī harī chē nāma
sadā mī bakti karū niṣkām

While doing the Lord's work, Lord Hari's name is always on my lips. My devotion is always without motive. My devotion of Lord Hari is always without any motive!

hṛdayāta dēva jasā pūṣpāta gandh
nātsat mī asā hōun dhūndh
āpaṇ tyāchē karūyā pūjan
śradhēnē nit nēmē vandan

The Lord dwells in the heart as fragrance in a flower. Bowing to Him with one-pointed concentration, let us pray to Him. We offer regular worship with utmost faith and devotion, without fail.

surēla gātē tyāchī muralī
gōp gōpinchī sudha būddha haralī
jagatāchī tō ādim śaktī
śōdhita phirtō viśuddha bhaktī

The lord's flute is so sweet and melodious that the gopas and gopis lost their consciousness. He is the power of the universe. He is ever wandering in search of pure devotion.

DĒVĀDIDĒVĀ (TELUGU)

dēvādidēvā ō mahādēvā
nīvē śaraṇayyā darijērcavayyā

O Lord of lords, O great Lord, we take refuge in You, take us to the goal.

jangamadēvarā janimṛtināśakā
mangaḷadāyakā amangaḷahārakā
kāḷahastīśvarā kalimalanāśakā
nīvē śaraṇayyā darijērcavayyā

O Lord of the ascetics with matted hair and ash-marks over their bodies, destroyer of birth and death, giver of auspiciousness and destroyer of inauspiciousness! Lord of Kalahasti, destroyer of evils of Kali Yuga (age of darkness) we take refuge in You, take us to the goal!

rakṣimpavayyā darijērcavayyā
nīvē śaraṇayyā

Protect us, take us to the goal, we take refuge in You.

bhūtagaṇanāthuḍā śavabhūmivāsuḍā
praṇavākāruḍā nīpraḷayakāruḍā
śrīśailavāsuḍā bhramarāmbanāthuḍā
nīvē śaraṇayyā darijērcavayyā

O Lord of ghouls (Shiva's companions), dweller of the cremation grounds, the form of the primordial sound Om, the cause of dissolution, Lord of Srisaila, Lord of Goddess Bramarambha, we take refuge in You, take us to the goal.

rakṣimpavayyā darijērcavayyā
nīvē śaraṇayyā

Protect us, take us to the goal, we take refuge in You.

duḥkhamayasāgaram dāṭimpavayyā
nī nāmamepuḍu pāḍedamayyā

Take us across this ocean of misery, we sing Your name always.

ōm namaḥ śivāya śiva ōm namaḥ śivāya
ōm namaḥ śivāya hara ōm namaḥ śivāya

Prostrations to Lord Shiva!

DĒVI DĒVI DĒVI (KANNADA)

trimūrttigaḷa īśvarī nīnu
trilōkagaḷa tāyi nīnu
trikālajñē dēvī nīnu
ī lōkadi ēkāsarē nīnu
dēvi dēvi ī manatumbi bā

O eternal Goddess, lord of the trinity, Mother of the three worlds, You know the three parts of time (past, present and future). You are the only refuge in this world. Oh Devi, come revel in my mind.

dēvi dēvi dēvi ī manatumbi bā
ninna mahime hāḍi hāḍi nā nalidāḍuvē

O Devi, come revel in my mind; I will sing and dance to Your glories.

sadākāla ninḍe dhyāna jīvakkilla samādhāna
nīnē nanagē gati amma nīnē nanna mahādēvī

Though always meditating on You, my mind is restless. You are my only refuge, You are my great Goddess.

antaranga bahiranga bhūta bhāvi vartamāna
paramasatya nīnē amma nīnē allavē mahākāḷī

Great Kali, supreme truth, You are everywhere – inside and outside. You are always there, in past, present and future.

trilōka pālini nīnu triguṇakāriṇi nīnu
viśvaśakti dēvī nīnu nīnē tāṇē mahāmayē

You are the protector of the three worlds, the cause of the three gunas, power of the universe, and the great illusory power.

mahādēvī mahākāḷī mahāmāyē nana tāyē
mahādēvī mahākāḷī mahāmāyē nana tāyē

My Mother, You are Mahakali, Mahadevi and Mahamaya.

DĒVĪ MAHĒŚVARĪ KĀḶĪ KARUṆĀKARĪ (KANNADA)

dēvī mahēśvarī kāḷī karuṇākarī
bandēmmā salahu banaśankarī
bandēmmā salahu banaśankarī
bandēmmā salahī bandhanavā biḍisi
kāyammā anavarata karuṇākarī

Devi, Maheshvari, Kali, Banashankari, She who is full of compassion, come and protect us. Remove us from bondage and protect us always, O Mother, full of compassion!

ninnaya bhakuti bhavadinda mukuti
iduvallave tāyi sariyāda yukuti
nīḍemage tāyē śuddhamatī
nityānityada yukuti nijabhakuti

Mother, isn't this the right path to have Your devotion, to find salvation from samsara? Mother, grant us pure wisdom, the proper discrimination between the eternal and the ephemeral, and true devotion.

mātā amṛtēśvarī durgā paramēśvari
mangaḷakāriṇi nīnammā
mangaḷakāriṇi jagadōddhāriṇi
pādakkē śaraṇu śaraṇammā

O Mother Amriteshvari, Durga, Parameshvari, You are the root of all auspiciousness. You are the uplifter of the world; I surrender at Your feet.

ammā, ammā, ammā, ammā
ammā ammā ennūtaliralī
smaraṇeyu usirige usirāgi irali
nāmasudhēyanu saviyalu tāyē
harasammā ninnī maguvannū

May I constantly chant "Amma,amma", may I constantly remember You with every breath. O Mother, bless this child of Yours to constantly enjoy the blissful nectar of Your name.

DURGGĒ Ī DHARE GIḶIDU BĀRĒ

(KANNADA)

durggē ī dhare giḷidu bārē
dēvi nī avatarisu bārē
tāyē ī manakomme bārē
kāḷi nī karuṇeyanu tōre

Durga, come down to earth. Devi, please incarnate here; Mother, come to my mind. Kali, show me Your compassion!

simhavāhini sahisenu nāninnu
manadali iruvā vāsanayā
ī manasina vāsane ṛakkasara
dhare giḷidu bārē duṣṭa samhāre
kāḷi nī karuṇeyanu tōre

I can't bear the burden of desires in my mind, O Simhavahini (She who rides upon a lion). O Destroyer of evil, please come down to earth to kill the desire demons of the mind. Kali, show me Your compassion!

triśśūladhāriṇi ambā bhavāni
bhaktara poreyuva bhavatāriṇi
bhaktiya nīṭu kāttyāyani
tāyē ī manakomme bārē
kāḷi nī karuṇeyanu tōre

O Mother Bhavani, who bears the trident, protects of the devotees, and rescues us from the ocean of transmigration. O Katyayani, please give me devotion. Mother, come to my mind; Kali, show me Your compassion!

ahaṅkārava bhēdisu bēganē
bhavapārumāḍu bhavatāriṇi
bhaktara hṛdayada mandākini
tāyē ī manakomme bārē
kāḷi nī karuṇeyanu tore

Mandakini of devotees' hearts, quickly destroy my ego and take me across the ocean of birth and death. Mother, come to my mind; Kali, show me Your compassion!

(Note: Mandakini is a heavenly river)

DUVIDHĀ DŪR KARŌ (HINDI)

duvidhā dūr karō jagadambē duvidhā dūr karō

O Mother of the universe, please remove my confusion.

viṣayōn mēin ham aisē uljhē
mukti ki kōyī rāh na sūjhē
rāh dikhāvō hamkō mātā
jay jagadambē mā jay jagadambē mā

We are trapped in the senses, unable to find our way to freedom. O Mother, please show us the path, remove our confusion.

jīvan kā sach samajh na pāyē
māyā mēm aisē bharmāyē
hamē bacālō hē jagadambē
jay jagadambē mā jay jagadambē mā

Our minds have been so submerged in delusion that we cannot understand our birth's real purpose. O Mother please save us from this ignorance.

jñān dhyān harī nām na pāyā
mānav hōkar janam gavāyā
cētan hōkar cēt na pāvūm
jay jagadambē mā jay jagadambē mā

We have neither gained knowledge, nor have we learned to focus our minds on You. We have wasted this human birth. Though awake, we lack the awareness of the divine presence. O Mother, please take away our confusion!

apnē kō jānā bas kāyā mēin –
mērā kā jāl baḍhāyā
bhavsāgar sē kēsē niklūn
jay jagadambē mā jay jagadambē mā

We are so focused on ourselves that we have forgotten our true nature. O Mother, You are the only one who can help us cross the ocean of selfishness.

nij ātmā sē huvā durāv
jahān dēkhūn tahān dūjā bhāv
dūjē sē kaisē ik jānū
jay jagadambē mā jay jagadambē mā

Whenever we drift away from our own Self, we feel separated from You. Please remove this veil of duality and help us to see the Oneness in all life.

is prapañc mēin kūch nahi apnā
lagtā phir bhi sac hē sapnā
bhūl bhulaiyā mē hūn bhaṭkā
jay jagadambē mā jay jagadambē mā

Though this world is illusion, it seems so real to us. We are lost in its maze. Please come and save us!

EK MĀGAṆE (MARATHI)

ek māgaṇe tujha jagadambe
ekkach deyī maj vardān
manī jāgavī aysī prītt
akhaṇḍa gave tū jhēch gīt

O Mother of the Universe, I ask for only one boon, that the flame of love for You always be lit in my heart. May every moment be spent singing Your praises.

nayanī rāhe tujhīchu mūrtti
śravaṇī paḍo tujhīchu kīrtti
jihvā gāvo tujhichu bhakti
hṛdayī rāho tujvar prīti

May Your divine form be always before my eyes. Wherever I may be, let me hear nothing but Your glories. May songs of devotion to You be ever on my lips. Let my heart be always filled with intense love for You.

kāyā vācā mane ghaḍāvī
akhaṇḍa sevā tujhīchu maulī
ek māgaṇe tujlā āyī
ek rūp hovo tav ṭhāyi

O compassionate Mother, may my body, mind, heart and words be ever engaged in serving You. O Mother, I ask for only one boon, that I may become one with You!

EÑCHI MAHIMENĀ (TULU)

eñchi mahimenā eñchi mahimenā
ammanā sthutiye namaka bhadaka kammenā
jagan nāthe pudaraga itte parvakālanā
appe bhaktiṭa kēṭa baramda panbi satyanā

What glory this is! The adoration of Mother fills our life with a divine fragrance. In this glorious time for the universe, one's devotion for Mother will drive away all evils.

olu kuṇṭa ōṭe pōṇṭa irena rūpane
irena rūpa nenada bhakti bhāv jinchiṇṭa
dēveroñchi dēveroñchi māta paṇ pera
sāra rūpa paṭeyinā appe dēvera

Wherever I go and whatever I gaze upon I see only Mother's form. The vision of that form has filled me with devotion. There is only one God; all of the different forms of God have merged in this form of the Goddess.

vīṇāpāṇi brahmanāṇi śāradāmbenē
Jīva ṭitti usuluṭuṇṭa appe gēnanē
sarvaśakti mahāmāyē jagadīśvarī
bhaktare gādēbatti divya śaktiye

Goddess, wife of Brahma (the creator), I offer my life to You. Goddess, You are the creative force of this universe. Those who follow You will benefit greatly from their devotion.

EṆCI PORUḶUDA (TULU)

eṇci poruḷuda telikkē appē
dairō diṇcinda baṇciḍu

What a beautiful smile You have, Mother! Seeing it, my heart is filled with courage.

pēru daṇcina abhaya dārē
manassu urkkuṇḍu bhaktiḍu

Your refuge comes to us as a protective flow. My mind is overflowing with devotion.

kaṣṭa naṣṭoru dūra pōppā
ninna nāmāda mahimeḍu

The greatness of Your name makes all difficulties and hardhips fly away.

dūṣṭa durittalu māyyā kāppā
amṛtattvōda nōṭṭōṭū

By granting me this nectar-filled sight of Your form, You are saving me from all evil, misery and illusion.

tyāga vairāgyō diṇci mūruti
saraḷa satguru īśvarī

You are the embodiment of renunciation and dispassion; You are my Satguru and Goddess.

kēṇḍi nēyin kai dērttu kōrppunā
mōkē diṇcina sumadhurī

You instantaneously and generously give us whatever we ask for. You are filled with love and supreme sweetness.

prēma śāntiddā bōḷppu kōrlē
bhakti ḍēnkulu sugippuvō

Grant us the light of love and peace. We will enjoy it in the fullness of bhakti.

appē īrēna prīti mayyippullē
jōkku lēnkulu nalīppuvō

O Mother, pour out Your love. We children will dance in bliss!

ENNAGA TARAMĀ (TELUGU)

ennaga taramā nī līlā
mati dāṭaga vaśamā nī māyā

Is it possible to understand Your divine play? Can the mind go beyond the veil of Your illusion?

jagamulanēlu trimūrttulakaina
tapamula dēlu munīsvarulainā
teliyagarānidi nī mahima
kanugona mēmenta vāramamma

Even Brahma, Vishnu and Shiva, who rule over the worlds, and great sages immersed in meditation, cannot comprehend Your greatness. O Mother, how can we behold Your splendor?

sṛṣṭisthitilaya kāriṇi nīvē
jīvana nāṭaka sūtradhāriṇivē
lōkapu rangasthalipai kadile
pātrala gamanāgamanamu nīvē

You are the creator, sustainer and destroyer of the universe. You direct the play of life and the movements of the characters on the stage.

velugu nīḍala kadalikalō
mūḍurangula kalayikalō
cāvupuṭṭukala valayamulō
cikkina bommala brōvagarāvō

We are trapped like puppets, caught in the play of light and darkness and the merging of the three gunas, ensnared in the cycle of birth and death. Please come and redeem us!

ē pēruna ninu pilicina nēmi
ē rūpunayeda kolicina gānī
ādiśaktivō mūlavirāṭṭuvō
ārttula kācē karuṇāmūrttivō

Whatever name we call You by, whatever form we worship You in, whether You are the primordial Shakti or the eternal Shiva, You are the compassionate one the protect the yearning souls.

ĒNU MĀḌALI (KANNADA)

ēnu māḍali enu māḍali ēnu māḍali ammā?
pūrṇṇavāgi kāṇalāre ninna bhavya rūpā
ēnu māḍali ammā?

What can I do Mother? I can't comprehend Your complete divine form. What can I do?

āliṅkana bayasi bandē ākatalla ayyō
vyōmavellā nīne āgihe entu hiḍiyalammā?
pūrṇṇavāgi kāṇalāre ninna bhavya rūpā
ēnu māḍali ammā?

I came to hug You Mother, but could not do so. You are as expansive as the universe, how can I hold You? Mother, what can I do?

nuṭiyalentu savimāṭu siddhavāgi bandē
ōmkāra sānidhyadi mūkaḷāki ninte
pūrṇṇavāgi kāṇalāre ninna bhavya rūpā
ēnu māḍali ammā?

I came prepared for sweet conversations, but was dumbfounded in Your divine presence. Mother, what can I do?

ēnu māḍali enu māḍali ēnu māḍali ammā?
ninna layikyavākatallate anyamārgavillā
ēnu māḍali ammā?

What can I do, Mother, what can I do? There is no other way other than becoming one with You. Mother, what can I do?

ninna layikya māṭikō

Please make me one with You!

ETAYŌ TĒṬI (TAMIL)

etayō tēṭi alaintu inṭru unai tēṭukirēn
kaṇmaṇiyē karuṇaimazhayē iruppiṭam tanai sol

All these years, I ran after worthless things. Today I look for the One who is full of compassion- please tell me where You live.

maunattil lakṣam pāṭhankaḷ tantāy
purintatellām appōt
sūzhnilai vantāl ellām marantēn
iggati toṭarntāl narggatiyuṇḍō?

Through silence, You teach me millions of lessons, and I understand it all quite clearly, but when new situations arise, I forget it all. Is it possible for me to progress with such a mind?

pāpangaḷ janmangaḷāyi sumantēn
inṭr tān bhāram enṭruṇarntēn
dēhattil sañcarittiṭumbōtē
bhārattai irakkiṭa mārggam kāṭṭu

For all of my previous births, I have been carrying a load of sins; only today did I realize that they are nothing but burdens. Show me the way to unburden myself of this weight while in this present body.

GAṆAṄGAḶIN NĀTHĀ (TAMIL)

gaṇaṅgaḷin nāthā kaitozhutōm
kavalaikaḷ tīrkka kaitozhutōm
guṇaṅgaḷin adhīpā kaitozhutōm
kuṭṭrankaḷ poruttiṭa kaitozhutōm

O Lord of divine beings, we worship You! We worship You, while seeking an end to our worries. O Lord of all good things, we worship You! We worship You that you may forgive our bad actions!

seyalkaḷai toṭankiṭa unai paṇivōm
jayankaḷai aruḷi kurai kaḷaivāy
uyyum vazhi tannai emakkuṇartta
uvappuṭan unnai kaitozhutōm

We surrender to You that you may give us strength to act. Grant us success in all that we do and correct our mistakes. Show us the correct path! We worship You with great sincerity.

kavalaikaḷ ellām tīrttiṭuvāy
kaṭum pakai tannai azhittiṭuvāy
abalaikaḷ enkaḷai kāttiṭave
anbarin tuṇaivā vandiṭuvāy

Remove all our worries, destroy the hatred that arises in our minds. O Savior of good people, please come and protect helpless ones like us!

ādimudalvanai ānaimukhattanai
aindkarattanai vaṇankiṭuvōm
vēdamudalvanai jñānakozhundinai
iruvinai nīnkiṭa vaṇankiṭuvōm – nām

You are the first leader and have an elephant face. You have five arms, and are the first knower of the Vedas. O quintessence of all knowledge! We worship You, that You may remove our bad karmas!

GAṆAPATI GUṆANIDHI (HINDI)

gaṇapati guṇanidhi tērē
guṇgāyak ham pyārē
sab vidhi tū rakhvārē
har lē duḥkh hamārē

O Lord Ganapati, You are the protector of Your devotees. We sing Your glories; please remove our sorrows.

gaṇapati karuṇā karnā tū
guṇanidhi sab var dētā tū
gajamukh mangaḷ bharnā tū
gaṇanāyak bhay harnā tū

O Lord Ganapati, treasure-house of compassion, O Lord Gunanidhi, bestower of boons, fill our lives with auspiciousness and remove our fears.

bahuvidha kaṣṭ mē paḍkē
din banē ham rōkē
ab tū rakṣak bankē
ājā gajmukh dōḍ kē

We are in deep sorrows; we are helpless. O Lord Ganapati, we are crying. Please come running and free us from the burden of sorrows.

sundar kajñara vadanā
jana par karuṇā karnā
muda mangal sab bharanā
tū karuṇā kā jharanā

You, Lord, who speaks beautifully, are the river of compassion. Grace us with Your compassion and bring prosperity to our lives.

girijā nandan var dē
pada vandana ham kartē
tērā yaś jō gate
unke bandhan miṭ tē

O Lord Ganapati, Son of Goddess Parvati, we worship Your lotus feet. We sing Your glories: please bless us that we may be freed from the bondage of worldly attachments.

GANGE GINTA (KANNADA)

gange ginta pavitralu nīnū ammā
hāliginta śubhravū ninna vadanā
yāva jaladi toleyali ninna pāda
oppisiko kaṇṇīra pāda majjanā

Mother, You are holier than the river Ganges. You are more fair than pure milk. With what water could Your feet be washed? Accept these tears with which I will wash Your feet.

sūrya ginta tējavu ninna nayanā
tāreginta kāntiyu ninna mūguti
yāv dīpadārati ettalammā
oppisiko kaṇgala nōṭṭadārati

Your eyes are brighter than the sun and Your nose ornament shines more resplendently than the stars. With what lamp could I perform arati to You? Accept my eyes, that gaze intently on Your form, with which I will perform arathi to You.

kamalakinta kōmala ninna karagalu
kusumakinta mōhaka ninna hūnagē
yāvahūva dindali ninna archana
oppisiko kaigala sēva puṣpava

Your hands are softer than a lotus. Your smile is more attractive than any type of flower. With what flower can I perform archana for You? Accept the work done by these hands as a substitute for the flowers offered to You in archana.

beṭṭakinta bhavyavu ninna svarūp
kaṭaliginta viśāla ninna maṭilu

yāva rūpadī nā ninna kāṇali
oppisiko hṛdayava ninna pādake

Your form is more glorious than the mountains; Your lap is wider than the sea. In what form can I visualize You? O Mother, accept my heart that I surrender at Your feet.

GIRIDHAR HĒ (HINDI)

giridhar hē yadunāth gōpālak
vrajapati mādhav śyam kalēbar
muraḷi bajākar ākar mōhan
madhumay rās racāvō radhēśyāṁ

O Lord who lifted the mountain, leader of the Yadavas, divine cowherd, Madhava! Come dance with us, play enchanting music on Your flute.

naṭvarlāl bihari manōhar
mōr mukuṭ dhar sundara manmatha –
kōṭi lajāvan muraḷi bajākar
āvō rās racānē śyām
rādhē śyām āvō rās racānē śyām

O beautiful One! wearing a crown adorned with a peacock feather, come dance with us! Radha Syam, come dance with us!

kāliyamardhan gōkulapālak –
gōpavadhūpriy hē madhusūdan
rādhāvallabh rāsēśvar hari
āvō rās racānē śyām
rādhē śyām āvō rās racānē śyām

You slew the demon Kaliya and protected the cowherds. You are the beloved of Radha and the Gopis, Lord of the rasa dance. Come dance with us, Radhe Syam, come dance with us!

māyāmanuṣ līlāvigrah
vēṇu vilōl viśālvilōcan
dēvakinandan dīnadayāmay
āvō rās racānē śyām
rādhē śyām āvō rās racānē śyām

Embodiment of the divine play, You play the flute and are the son of Devaki. You are compassionate to the downtrodden. Come dance with us, Radhe Syam, come dance with us!

HARA ŌM ŚIVA (KANNADA)

hara ōm śiva ōm hara ōm namaśivāya

Salutations to Lord Shiva!

hariyuva nadiyā kalaravadalli
kēḷutaliruvudu śivanāma
raghava rāmana hṛdayada miḍita
āgihudallavē haranāma

In the sound of the flowing river, Lord Siva's chants are heard; in the heart beat of Raghava Rama, the chant is created.

kaṇa kaṇadallū ā śivanē
ramisihanaiyyā jagadoḷagē
śiva śiva bhajisalu ō manavē
kāṇuvē śivananu yalleḍegē

Lord Shiva is reveling in every atom. Chant that supreme mantra, O man, and you will see Rama everywhere.

nānu nannadu enaiyyā
śivatānellavu tiḷiyaiyyā
śivanē guruvu nōḍaiyyā
guruvē śivanu ariyaiyyā

What is there to say "I" or "mine? Everything belongs to Lord Shiva. Again know that Lord Shiva is the teacher.

HARE PĀṆḌURANGA (MARATHI)

hare pāṇḍuranga paṇḍarināthā
hare vāsudeva rakumāyināthā
vaikuṇtha vāsā purandara viṭṭhala
meghaśyāma puṇdalīka varadā

Victory to Lord Panduranga, the guardian of Pandaripura. Victory to the son of Vasudeva, Lord of Rukmini, who resides in heaven and whose complexion is like that of a dark rain-cloud.

japū yā karū yā kṛṣṇa nāma ghevū yā
bhajan karū yā japan karū yā
hariche nām ghevū yā kṛṣṇa nām ghevū yā
kṛṣṇa nām ghevū yā (hare pāṇḍuranga x 8)

I repeat, I think, I sing the names of Lord Krishna. Chant Lord Hari's name, chant Lord Krishna's name, victory to Lord Panduranga!

pāṇḍuranga rakumāyi nāthā
pāṇḍuranga trilokanāthā
pāṇḍuranga vaikuṇtha vāsā

pāṇḍuranga muktidātā
pāṇḍuranga purandara viṭṭhalā
pāṇḍuranga paṇḍarināthā

Lord Panduranga, Lord of Rukmini, Lord of the three worlds, who dwells in Vaikuntha, who bestows liberation, Vitthala, who stands on a brick, Lord of Pandaripura.

HARĒ TŪ HAMĀRĒ (HINDI)

harē tū hamārē
hṛdaya kō curākē
virah kī agan mē
hame kyō jalātā

O Lord Hari, You have stolen our hearts. Why do You burn us in the fire of separation?

hare kṛṣṇa śaurē
vibhō viśvamūrttē
mukundā murārē
yaśōdā kē pyārē

O Lord Krishna, Lord of the universe, destroyer of the demon Mura, You are the darling son of Yashoda.

kabhī bānsurī mē
madhura tān chēṭakē
lubhātā tū hamkō
dars tō na dētā

You enchant us by playing sweet music on Your divine flute, but You never show us Your divine form.

niṭhūr hōkē dilsē
madhur muskurātā

nacātā hē apanē
īśārē par sabkō

You have become so uncaring, and yet, You smile at us and make us dance at Your command.

nichāvar hē mādhav
pagōm par ham cākar
hamē tū na chōḍnā
abhī āke milnā

O Madhava, this servant of Yours is an offering at Your lotus feet. Please do not leave us, come and grant us the vision of Your divine form.

HARI BŌL HARI BŌL (HINDI)

hari bōl hari bōl hari bōl hari bōl
hari bōl hari hari bōl (2x)

Sing and chant the name of Hari.

śyāma varṇṇā sundarāngā
rādhikā samētā
vāsudēvā vēṇu lōlā
rāsa kēli lōla (2x)

Your handsome body is of a dark blue complexion. O son of Vasudeva, master of the flute, with Radha at Your side You enjoy the dance of the Gopis.

yādavēndrā nandalālā
kāmakōṭi ramyā
mañju hāsā mānasēśā
mādhavā murārē (2x)

O Lord of the Yadavas, son of Nanda, You blissfully reside beyond the reach of desire. O Lord of the mind, blessed with a beautiful smile, You destroyed the demon named Mura.

patmanābhā pītachēlā
pāhimām ramēśā
gōkulēśā gōpabālā
gōpa vṛnda nāthā (2x)

Lord Vishnu, adorned in yellow clothing, Lord of Lakshmi, grant us refuge. Lord of Gokula, cowherd boy, You are the Lord and protector of the cowherd children.

viśva rūpā vēda vēdyā
tvat padābjam vandē
dēva dēva dīn nāthā
dēhi mamgalam mē (2x)

Your true form encompasses the universe and Your knowledge encompasses the whole of the Vedas. I prostrate before Your lotus feet. You are the Lord who grants refuge to the downtrodden. Grant me auspiciousness.

HARI NĀRĀYAṆA (HINDI)

hari nārāyaṇa jaya nārāyaṇa
hari nārāyaṇa gōvinda

Glory to Lord Narayana, Glory to Lord Govinda.

brahmā viṣṇu śiv man bhāvan
jaya nārāyaṇ hari nārāyaṇ

He is dear to Lord Brahama, Vishnu, and Shiva. Glory to Lord Narayana!

gangā yamuna caraṇ pakhāraṇ
bhav sāgar kē pār utāraṇ

The holy rivers Ganga and Yamuna worship His feet. He helps His devotees cross the ocean of transmigration.

khud bichṭāvan khud mil āvan
khud taṭpāvan khud darśāvan

He draws close to the devotees, and then moves away; He causes suffering and also removes it.

dīn duḥkhī kē dukh apnāvan
bhīr pare tō dhīr baṇdhāvan

He supports the weak and suffering. He consoles those who are downtrodden. He is loved and glorified by His devotees.

jap tap kē bhi pakaṭ na āvan
pyār pukārē dōṭē āvan

By singing His glories, we may reach the state of happiness. He cannot be bound by japa and tapas.

tan man gāvan jan jan gāvan
gāvan gāvan sab sukh pāvan

However, He will come running to you if you call Him with love and devotion.

HĒ GAṆANĀYAKA SIDDIVINĀYAKA

(MARATHI)

hē gaṇanāyaka siddivināyaka
mangala mūrti svāmi
gaṇādhīśā tū guṇadhīśa tū
varada vināyaka namō namaḥ

O Leader of the ganas, Lord Siddhivinayaka, bestower of success. You are the embodiment of auspiciousness, You are the ruler of the hosts, You are the embodiment of good qualities.We bow to You, Lord Varada Vinayaka, bestower of boons.

hē girijātmaja buddhipradāyaka
vighnaśvara jay sankaṭ nāśaka
sūkhakaratā tū dukhaharatā tū
viśva vināyaka namō namaḥ

O Son of Goddess Girija, bestower of intelligence, Victory to You lord Vighneswara, (remover of obstacles) who destroys misery. You are the Lord who bestows happiness and removes sorrows; we bow to You, Lord Vishva Vinayaka, Lord of the universe.

hē cintāmaṇi śubha phala dāyaka
ballāḷēśvara jay viśvēśvara
lambōdara tū sarvēśvara tū
sanmatī dāyaka namō namaḥ

O fulfiller of all desires, bestower of good, victory to You, Lord Ballalesvara, (who saved Ballala), Lord of the universe. You are the pot bellied Lord, You are the Lord of all, we bow to You, who bestows a good intellect.

hē mahāgaṇāpati pāpavināśaka
ganēśvara jay vighnavināśaka
mayūrēśvara tū paramēśvara tū
aṣṭavināyaka namō namaḥ

O Lord Mahaganapati, destroyer of sins, victory to You, Lord Ganeshwara, the Lord of ganas and Lord Vighnavinayaka, destroyer of obstacles. You ride the peacock, You are the Supreme Lord, we bow to You, Lord Ashtavinayaka.

HĒ NANDALĀLĀ TUHJĒ (HINDI)

hē nandalālā tuhjē
ḍhūnḍhē braj bālā
śyām gōpālā – kānhā (x2)
śyām gōpālā

I search for You son of Nanda, lad of Braj.

mākhan chōr tūnē dil mērā churāyā
prīt na jānī mērē śyām gōpālā
śyām gōpālā mērē śyām (x2)

Stealer of butter, You have stolen my mind. O dark cowherd, You have stolen my mind.

kahē brij bālā mē nē kāhē dil lagāyā
kahā chipē hō mērē nandā kē lālā

Why O why did I lose my heart, where are You hiding, O my Krishna?

muralī kī dhun sun kahē braj bālā
darśan dēdō mērē kṛṣṇa gōpālā
śyām śyām bōlē mērā kaṇ kaṇ rē
mērā man rē mērā man rē
tū hī mērē jīvan kā ādhār rē

Hearing the sound of the flute this child of Braj says, "let me have Your darshan." Every part of my being and my mind calls out "Shyam, Shyam!". You are the only support in my life.

śyām rūp prēm rūp jay līlā dhām kī
gōp sang prēm rang jay bōlō śyam kī

Victory to the One with a dark form, the form of love, the home of the cosmic play. Victory to the One who enacts the dance of divine love with the gopis.

HŌLŌ NA ŚŌMĀY (BENGALI)

hōlō na śōmāy ēkhōnō tōr?
śōmāy kēṭē jāy jībōnē mor
hōy janō mā āśā pūrṇō
mōn jyanō kādē tōrī jonnō

Do you still have no time for me? My life is wasted. Please fulfill my desire; I keep crying for You.

hṛdōy janō ṣōpitē pārī
māyār khēlāy janō na hārī
śiṅhōbāhinī bōlē tōrē ṣōbē
pārī janō tōr śiṅhō hōtē

Please ensure that I can offer You my heart, and won't be defeated by Maya's play. They call You Simhavahini (the one riding on a lion); I would like to be Your Simha (lion)!

tōrī kṛpā cāy mā amī
doyā kōriṣ mā doyāmoyī
bōlō kī lābh dērī kōrē?
tōrī kāchē jētē hōbē mōrē

I seek only Your grace. Be kind, Dayamayi (one full of kindness). What do You gain by waiting? I have to be with You only, after all.

āchiṣ kōthāy dē mā bōlē
kōtō ār khūñjī ēyi bhūtōlē

lāgē bhōy tōr ōy bhōyonkar rūp
rōktim khāḍā dēkhē kēpē ōṭhē būk

Please let me know where You are. I've searched for so long all over the earth. I'm frightened of Your fierce form, scared of Your blood-smeared sword!

bēd purāṇ mā ṣōbī tōr kōlē
cōl mā nīyē alōr dēśē
śvēt bośōnē elī mā kāḷī
hṛdi kōmōlē bōṣō omṛtēṣorī

The Vedas and Puranas all live in You. Take me to the world of light. Oh Mother, You've come this time dressed in white. Oh eternal goddess, please come and sit in the lotus of my heart.

HṚDAY MĀ (GUJARATI)

hṛday mā lāvō rām nē tame
jīvan banāvō ayōddhyā dhām
rām nām nō jāp karī lō
chōḍō tārā mārānō bhāv

Invite Rama into your heart, transform your life into Ayodhya (a place where there is no war). Abandoning all feelings of 'yours' and 'mine', chant Rama's name always!

sagā sambandhī nāthē nahī āvē
nahī āvē chōkrā chaiyā rē
sāthē tārī nām rāmnu
bhajīlē man tū rāmnu nāṁ
śrī rām jay rām jay jay rām jay
śrī rām jay rām jay jay rām

Relatives and friends will not remain by your side, nor will your children. Only Lord Rama's name will stay with you! O mind, chant the name of Rama, victory to Lord Rama!

rāṁ nāmthi patthar tarē
āppaḷē tarīyē bhavpār rē
rām nāmnō mahimā apār
bhajīlē man tū rāmnu nām
śrī rām jay rām jay jay rām jay
śrī rām jay rām jay jay rām

Bearing Lord Rama's name, even rocks can float on water. Chanting His name, we will cross the ocean of samsara (the cycle of life and death). The glory of Rama's name is infinite and without equal. O mind, chant the name of Rama, victory to Lord Rama!

vānar man nē rām mā vāḷō
layī jāśē lankā pār rē
rām nāmthī banyā hanumān
rām bhakt hanumān rē
śrī rām jay rām jay jay rām jay
śrī rām jay rām jay jay rām

Turn your monkey mind towards Ram. He will take you across Lanka, the land of maya. Chanting His name made Hanuman Lord Rama's dearest devotee.

HUṀ TŌ MĀ MAIN TĒRĀ HĪ (HINDI)

huṁ tō mā main tērā hī
mujhe kabhi na karnā tyāg
arth he kyā is jīvankā
yadi tērā nā hō sāth

O Mother I am Yours only. Never abandon me. What meaning is there to life, if You are not by my side?

chañchal asthir man hē mērā
tērā rūp main dēkh na pāvuṅ
ahaṁkār sē andhā huṅ
tērē prēṁ kō samajh nā pāvuṅ

My mind is fickle, always wandering. I am unable to see Your form. Blinded by ego, I cannot even comprehend Your love.

mēri puṇya kī jhōli khāli hai
pāp kā bhāṇd bahu bhāri hai
jap tap dyān me adhūrā huṅ
māyā mōh me ḍūbā huṅ

The pouch of my merits is empty but the sack of sins is heavy. Ignorant of meditation, japa and penance, I am submerged in illusory attachments.

nanhā huṅ main akēla huṅ
chōḍā jag ne sāth mērā
ēk aise mōḍ pē āyāhuṅ
jahāṁ chārō ōr he andhērā
taḍpā huṅ mēṁ tarasā huṅ
tērē amṛt prēm kā pyāsā
mayyā tēri kṛpā dṛṣṭi sē
kar dēnā ujiyārā

I am still young and alone, everyone in this world has left my company. I have reached the stage where there is nothing but darkness on all four sides. I am longing and thirsting for Your eternal love. O Mother, fill my life with Your love and eternal light. Please come to quench my thirst!

kar dēnā ujiyārā maiyyā

O Mother, please enlighten my life!

INIYEṆU KĀṆUM (MALAYALAM)

iniyeṇu kāṇum kamanīya rūpam
tirayumen mānasattil nīri
piḍayumen mānasattil
mayaṅgunna pakalinde maḍittaṭṭil talacāycu
mayaṅgumen mānasattil!

My mind is burning and writhing for Your darshan – when will I again see Your beautiful form? My mind is sleeping in the lap of the day that is itself dozing.

svapnamanōmaya naśvarabhūmiyil
niḥsvanāy ñānalaññu
nityanirāmayī , svapnaṅgaḷokkeyum
mithyayāy ñānariññu!

With a mind full of dreams, I wandered without any possessions in this perishable world. O Mother, eternal One, free from all sorrow - I have seen that all dreams are unreal.

cañcalamānasa nombaravīṇatan
tantriyilīṇamākū
cintayil nin mahāmantravumāyi ñān
venteriyuṇu dūre!

Mother, please become a melody on the strings of my mind's veena which is unsteady and full of pain. I am repeating Your great mantra in my mind and burning in sorrow.

satvaramen manaḥ nirjjalabhūmiyil
sargaparjjanyamākū

cinmayī, nin kazhal nityapūjaykkende
cittatārōṇṇu mātram!

Please come quickly as rain in the parched land of my mind. O Mother, who is supreme consciousness, I have only the flower of my heart to offer in the daily worship of Your holy feet.

IŚVAR PARAMEŚVARĀ (HINDI)

iśvar parameśvarā umā maheśvarā
jagadīśvarā jagadiśvarā harahara śankarā

Praise to Lord Shiva, the supreme, Uma's lord, Lord of the universe!

śiva śiva harahara śiva śiva hara hara
śiva śiva harahara śiva śiva hara hara
śiva śiva śiva śiva śiva śiva śiva śiva śankarā
dekhiye dekhiye humko

O Lord, please look towards us!

praṇām hāmare svīkār kījiye
dekhiye dekhiye humko
vardān humko dījiye

Please look at us! Accept our prostrations, gaze upon us and bestow Your blessings!

śankarā abhayankarā śankarā abhayankarā
śankarā abhayankarā śankarā abhayankarā
śivaśambho mahādevā śankarā

Glory to Shiva, Shambo, Shankara, the great god, the remover of fear!

JAI GAṆĒŚA JAI ĒKADANTA (HINDI)

jai gaṇēśa jai ēkadanta
jai lambōdara viṣṇō
jai mahēś sut pārvati nandana
jai vighnēś vibhō

Victory Ganesha, who is beyond dualitie, who is ever content, omnipresent, son of Shiva and Parvati, divine One, who removes obstacles

vighna rāj tum bhīmakāy tum
dē dō vijay hamē
praṇav rūp tum vakratuṇd tum
ham kō tum vara dō

Lord of obstacles, with a huge body and a curved trunk, formed like the Sacred OM, grant me victory.

svarṇa varṇ tum dēva pūjy tum
mūṣikavāhan tum
dharma buddhi dō divya dhriṣṭi dō
sarva vighna har tum

Golden hued, worshipped by the gods, with a mouse (representing desire) as a vehicle. Grant me righteous thinking and divine vision, and remove all obstacles.

JAI JAI JANANĪ JAI HŌ TERĪ (HINDI)

jai jai jananī jai hō terī
jai bhavataraṇī bhagyavidhātrī
jai śivaramanī mātabhavānī
jai bhayaharanī dēvi mahēśī
jai jai mā

Victory to You Mother, victory to one who takes us across the ocean of birth and death, to the one ordains our fate, the beloved of Lord Shiva, the one who removes fear! Victory to Mother, victory to Mother!

tum hī mērā sab kuch mayyā
muj par karuṇā tum ab karnā
tum sabkī hō pyārī jananī
dūr karō sab sankaṭ jaldī
jai jai mā

Mother, You are my everything. Please show mercy to me now. Mother, You are the beloved of all; kindly remove all sorrows soon! Victory to Mother, victory to Mother!

divya mahātbhut mayyā tērī
sṛṣṭi-sthiti-lay rūpī līlā
dēv munīśvar dās tumhāre
daitya tumhārē bal sē hārē
jai jai mā

Your divine play of creation, maintenance and dissolution of this universe is a great wonder, Mother! All the celestials and the sages are Your servants. All the demonic beings have been destroyed by Your force. Victory to Mother, victory to Mother!

bhaktajanōn kō kalpalatā – sam
vānchit var sab dētī hō tum
ham sab tērā nām pukārē
dūr karō sab duhkh hamārē
jai jai mā

You fulfill all the desires of Your devotees like the legendary wish-fulfilling creeper. We are calling out Your name! Kindly remove all our sorrows. Victory to Mother!

JAY JANANĪ (HINDI)

jay jananī jagajananī māte
terā stavan karun me
jay girirājakumāri maheśi
jay jagadamba bhavāni

Glory to the Mother, glory to the Mother of the universe! I sing Your praises. Glory to the daughter of Giriraja! Glory to the great Goddess, the Mother of the universe!

jay mahiṣāsuramardini jay jay
jay girivāsini jay jay
jay ripubhīti vibhanjini jay jay
jay karuṇāmayi jay jay

Glory to the slayer of the demon Mahishasura, glory to She who dwells in the mountain! You remove the fear of our enemies. Glory to You, embodiment of compassion!

durgatihāriṇi durgama rupiṇi
durge devi namaste
duṣṭāntaki he duḥkhanivāriṇi
dīnon par kar karuṇā
kar karunaa ham pe

I salute You who removes all misfortunes and takes the form of Mother Durga. Salutations to You, the remover of pain. You destroy evil; be compassionate towards us!

aṣṭabhujā tū navadurgā tū
aṣṭaiśvarya vidhātrī

āṭhom yām tujhī me maiyā
līn rahe man merā

You have eight arms, and take nine forms (the nine forms of Durga). You bestow upon us the eight types of prosperity. The eight parts of the day are contained within You. May my mind dissolve in You!

līlālole bandhan – mokṣh
sabhī he līlā terī
māyā brahm sabhī tū hī he
tū he sab se nyārī

O playful one! Entangling us in maya, and breaking us free from its clutches: both are Your play! You are both maya and the supreme Brahman. You are most extraordinary, Mother!

JÑĀNAKKAṬALTANNAI (TAMIL)

jñānakkaṭaltannai mīn aḷakkalāmā
aḷakkintra potu sirikkintrāy tāyē
mīn sintum kaṇṇīrkkaṭal sērumō
sirumīnin kaṇṇīrkku vazhi sollumō?

Can an ignorant fish measure the depth of the ocean of knowledge? If it tries at all, O Devi, You laugh at its attempts. Will the tears of this fish reach the ocean? Will Devi, knowledge personified, offer a solution?

unnai tēṭi aṭaya uḷ nōkkumbōtu
alaimōtum eṇṇankaḷ taṭam māttrakkūṭum
īrkkintra śaktivaṭivāna ammā
varavēṇḍum varavēṇḍum nizhalāka dēvī

As I wander in search of You, unwanted thoughts may come and distract me, pulling me in another direction. O, She who attracts the masses! Come and stay with me like a protective shadow.

uyirōṭu uyirāka kalantiruppāyē
kaikūppi siram tāzhtta kaṇ pārppāyē
sodanaikaḷ tantu āzham pārkkintrāy
padam pārttu nal bhakti nalkukintrāy

When I bow in reverence, remaining as one with the Soul, You glance at me with love and compassion. To check the intensity of my search, You test me in different ways, and then grant me pure bhakti.

JÑĀNAYŌGA ARIVUMILLAI (TAMIL)

jñānayōga arivumillai
karmayōga tuṇivumillai
bhaktiyōga anbumillai
pādantanai pattri ninḍrēn

I have not the knowledge for Jnana yoga (the yoga of discrimination), nor the courage for Karma Yoga (the yoga of service). I have no love for Bhakti Yoga (the yoga of devotion) – all I can do is hold on to Your feet!

pakuttariya niranumillai
paṭṭarivu siritumillai
kaṭṭrarivum koñcamammā
kāliraṇḍum tañcamammā

My memory is poor, I have no talent for music, I have had little schooling – my only refuge is Your two feet!

tāyaḍikkum kāraṇankaḷ
tānariyā kuzhantaiyammā
tāy mukhattai pārttu vimmum
tanayan tuyar tīrttiḍammā

I am a child who does not know the reasons for Your tests. Mother! Please console this child's sorrow, this child who cries when he gazes upon You!

śaraṇam śaraṇam śaraṇam ammā
un tiruppādam śaraṇam ammā
śaraṇam śaraṇam śaraṇam ammā
un tiruppādam śaraṇam ammā

Grant me refuge at Your feet, Mother!

KAB ĀYE GĀ (HINDI)

kab āye gā vō din prabhujī
chabi tērī dēkh pāvū me
param prēm kē gangā jal me
har pal nahāvūm me

O Lord, when will that day come when I will see Your image? When I will bathe every moment in the holy Ganges water of eternal love?

tērē vacanō kō suntē prabhujī
bhāv vibhōr hō jāvūn me
man mandir kē vṛndāvan me
divya rās racāvūn me

O Lord, when will I be overcome with love while listening to Your words? When will I perform the diving dance in the Vrindavan of my mind?

ahankār kī ghōr pakad se
mukt hō jāvūn mē
tērē hāthō me basūm prabhujī
tērī bānsuri ban jāvūm me

When will I be free from the strong hold of the ego? It will come to be when, in Your hands, I become Your flute.

prēm kā ras pān karke
prēm hī ban jāvūn me
sāgar me jese saritā mile
tujh me ghulmil jāvūn me

Drinking the nectar of love, when will I become love itself? When will I become one with You, as the river merges into the ocean?

KAḌALŌRAM (TAMIL)

kaḍalōram tavam seyyum kāḷiyammā
kanivōḍu emai kākkum śaktiyammā
maḍal virikkum malarkal ena bhakti veḷḷam
maṇ padaiyil pāycukintra śaktiyammā
kāḷiyammā enkaḷ dēviyammā

Mother Kali, who meditates on the seashore, Shakti Amma compassionately protects me. As a flower unfolds its petals, Shakti Amma removes the dirt with the water of devotion. O Mother Kali! Our divine Mother!

piravi enum kaṭal kaṭakka tōṇi āvāy
pirppaṭṭōr nalam peravē ēṇi āvāy
marati enum mayakkattai pōkkiṭuvāy
manatil irai chintanaiyai vaḷattiṭuvāy

kāḷiyammā enkaḷ dēviyammā

May You become the boat that carries us accross the ocean of transmigration. May You become the ladder to uplift the downtrodden. May You remove the dizziness of our forgetfulness. May thoughts of You grow in my heart.

uravu solli tiruvaḍiyai pattri nirppōr
uyarvaḍaiya varam taruvāy enḍrum ammā
turaviyarum pōttrukinḍra tūyavaḷē
teviṭṭāta pērinbam tarupavaḷē
kāḷiyammā enkaḷ dēviyammā

You grant boons that uplift whoever takes refuge in You and calls You their own. The monks and sadhus also praise You as the pure one. O Mother Kali, You are the giver of bliss, our divine Mother!

KĀLATTIN PUSTAKAM (MALAYALAM)

kālattin pustakattāḷin ñān – ennē
kurichiṭṭatāṇende svapnam
nēriyōrōrmmatan vātsalyamāṇende
nērākum ammayām svapnam

I have written my sweet dreams in the book of Time: the faint memory of genuine motherly affection.

kaṇṇīr tūki nin pādattilettavē
kāruṇyavarṣattilenne
pērttum kuḷippichu mārōṭaṇachu nī
puṇcirippaimbālumēki

When I reached Your feet, tears flowing from my eyes, You embraced me again and again, showering me with compassion. You held me close to Your heart, Your smile as pure as fresh milk.

vīṇḍum tiriññonnu nōkkavē nin mizhi
enniluṇḍennu ñān kaṇḍu
viṅi vitumbi ñān ammē virahattin
vēdanayuṇḍennil innum

When I looked back, I saw You gazing upon me. Today I still sob with the pain of separation from Mother.

nitya vasantamāy nirmala prēmamāy
nityavum ennil vasikkū
ā prēmapīyuṣa sāgaram nukarnnu ñān
ā divyadhāmamēriṭaṭṭe

Come and dwell in me forever, as eternal springtime, as immaculate divine love. Then I will taste that ocean of nectar of Your pure love. Let me climb to that divine abode.

KĀḶI MAHEŚVARIYE (MALAYALAM)

kāḷi maheśvariye – jaganmāte
kaitozhām endeyamme!
nintiru cinta cintum – viśva bhramam
entoru jālamamme!

O Kali! Goddess of the universe! My salutations to You. This whole world is merely a thought of Yours. O Mother! What an enchanting world!

vālum talayumilla – prapaṇcattin
veru nīyennukelppū
entoru bhrāntu tāye – satyāsatyam

kīzhmel marichiṭunnu

They say that You are the root of the universe, that has neither head nor tail. O Mother, what craziness! You turn both truth and untruth upside down!

brahmānandam kuṭichu - madichīṭum
nin viśvakeḷikaḷil
yuktikanḍettiṭamo - chāyāmayī
nin līlayentu bhrāntu!

You drink absolute bliss! Can anyone see logic in Your divine universal play? Your divine play itself is confusion!

ādyantahīnamākum - māyāvastram
neytukūṭṭunnatāye
svantamaraykku cuttum - śatru hastam
ñāttunnatentu citram!

What a picture! You hang the hands of enemies around Your waist and stitch the cloth of illusion, which has neither beginning nor end.

tārakaratnajālam - koruttiṭum
viśvavidhāyikaykku
naramuṇḍamāla mātran - mahāmāye
citram vicitramamme!

You weave the fate of the universe as You have weaved the gem-like stars into the sky, O Goddess of illusion! You hang a garland of skulls around your neck, how wonderful is Your vision!

paṇcabhūtagṛhangaḷ - paṭuttiṭum
bhairavī viśva śiḷppi
kālu kuttān kulame - labhikkāte
nī vasippū śmaśāne

O Bhairavi! You are the architect of the universe! The houses of five elements are made by You. Since You could find nowhere to place Your feet, You reside in the graveyard!

āṇpeṇ napumsakavum – allennālum
peṇkolam keṭṭiyāṭum
peṇkolam keṭṭiyiṭṭum – śumbhādikaḷ
kālanāy naṇṇi ninne

Though You are neither male, nor female, nor genderless, You enact Your play in a female form. Though You have this female form, demons like Sumbha regarded You as the 'God of Death.'

malinam kṣaṇikamāmī – śarīrattil
bhramamārnna mānavaril
'ñān' kemanenne bhāvam – vechukaṭṭi
tuḷḷikkum kaḷḷi nīye!

Humans are illusioned by the impure and fleeting body; You are the thief who makes humans dance by implanting the thought 'I am Great!' in them.

oro nimeṣameṇṇi – incincāyi
cattu tulayuvoril
'hanta! ñānum tulayum' enna cinta
nalkāttoramme tozhām

Inch by inch, people are dying every moment. I salute You who does not give us the thought that 'I will also perish'.

pokumboḷ koṇḍu pokām – oru cilli
polumillenkilum hā!
koṭikaḷ kūṭṭiṭunna pariṣaye
viḍḍikeṭṭippatum nī!

At the time of death, nobody takes even a penny along with them. Yet You make foolish humans strive to earn crores.

pettunovūttamettam – pakṣe sadā
pettukkūṭṭunnu pattam
cettattam yogyatapol tonnippikkum
nin līla tanne līla!

Even though labor pains are horrible, people continue to give birth. Seeing Your play, one would feel that callousness is one of Your qualities.

nāṇameśātta kāḷī – ninakkāru
cekkane tanniṭunnū
nityavum kanyakayāy naṭannoḷū
dvandvamillātta kemī!

O Kali, who had no sense of shame, who would give You a guy? O great one, who are non-dual in nature, continue as a virgin!

nīyallātārulakil – parāpare
nīyillātāranangum
brahmavum mūrttikaḷum calikkunna
śakti nin śakti tannē!

Other than You, who else is there in the universe? O supreme one, who can move without you? Your power is the power behind Brahma and the devas.

omkāram aimkāravum – hrīmkāravum
klīmkāram śrīmkāravum
sarva bijangaḷum nī gāyatriyum
vedamavedavum nī

You are the primordial sound, Om. You are the hrimkara, kleemkara and sreemkara. You are the seed of everything, Gayatri, the Vedas and the scriptures.

kāḷī karāḷi rudre – jhilam jhilam
tuḷḷutullende kāḷī
triguṇangaḷkkappuram nin kalāśangaḷ
āru kāṇunnu tāye

O Kali, Karali, consort of Rudra, dance! Dance, making the sound 'jhilam! jhilam!' O Mother! Who can see Your divine play beyond the three attributes?

triputiyum poṭiyāyiṭum – cidākāśam
śatakoṭi jyotirggaṇam
sahasrārattilāṇḍu – madampoṭṭi
ninnuraññārkkumamme

As You dance, intoxicatedly centered in the Sahasrara, the triputis (knowledge, knower and known) are powdered and You churn the infinite universe into thousands of milkyways.

inningu nāḷeyangu – ninneteṭi
sādhakar paññiṭunnu
nī kiṭannoṭiṭunnu – turīyavum
ārettum ninde kūṭe

Seekers rush here and there in search of You. You who run beyond turiya! Who can reach You?

jyotirmayam anantam – śāntidhāmam
ānanda sāgarāntam
sachidānandasāndram – jñānaghanam
ninde lokam maheśī!

O Goddess of the Universe! Your abode is eternal light, abode of peace and ocean of bliss. It is full of sat-chit-ananda, and dense with knowledge.

addivyadyovilettum – ninnoṭoppam
ottu nṛttam caviṭṭum
om kāḷi bhadrakāḷi japichuñān
ninpiḷḷatuḷḷum amme!

I will reach Your divine world and dance with You. Chanting Your name, I will dance with You as Your child.

māyāmayam anityam – duḥkhapradam
īlokam veṇḍatāye
ā lokam ninde lokam – ettum vare
nin nāmam ñān japikkum

I don't want this illusory, transient world full of sorrow. Until I reach Your world, I will chant your divine name.

ā nāmam divyanāmam – japichu ñān
bhaktiyil mungum amme
śuddha bhaktikku mātram anugraham
nalkuken ponnutāye!

O Mother, chanting Your divine name, I will become immersed in devotion! O my beloved Mother, please grant the boon to have only pure devotion.

kāli maheśwariye- maha māye
śri bhadrakali rudre
candi cāmundi durge- kartyāyani
kaitozhām ende amme

O Kali, great Goddess of this illusory world, auspicious one, consort of Rudra! Salutations to You who slayed the demons Chanda and Munda, O Mother Durga, Katyayani!

śāmbhavi loka māte śivankari
śankari śakti rupe
kālarātri karāli- kapālini
kaitozham ende amme

Salutations to the consort of Sambhu, the mother of the universe, who bestows auspiciousness, who is supreme power Herself. Kalaratri, who wears a garland of skulls, I salute You!

KĀLKAḶ NAḌUṄKA (TAMIL)

kālkaḷ naḍuṅka dēhaṁ ōyntu oḍuṅkuṁ
– nēraṁ ninaivirukkumō
jīvan tannai marakkumō
atanāl inṭrē nān solli vaittēn
namō nārāyaṇā namō nārāyaṇā
namō nārāyaṇā

Will I remember You when my body tires and weakens, legs trembling? Will I forget You at that state? - hence I hasten and chant Your name today itself.

manaṁ ōṭuṁ ōṭṭaṁ ninṭru
ezhuṁ iṭattil aṭaṅkumō
karmmavinai kaṭanpaṭṭu
nīnḍa payaṇaṁ toḍarumō
kālaṁ muzhutuṁ kūvi azhaikka
rōmaṁ kūḍa nāmaṁ solluṁ nārāyaṇā
namō nārāyaṇā namō nārāyaṇā
namō nārāyaṇā

Will the mind pause from its fast pace, and allow the real Self to arise? Will the soul's long journey continue this way, weighed down by the results of past actions? If one chants the Lord's name aloud for the whole of one's life, the very hair of the body will chant the name 'Narayana'.

pērpukazhil mayaṇkiviṭṭāl
vasaimozhiyāl taḷarvatuṁ
samanilaiyil manaṁ nirutta
akattūymai tēvayē
āḍippāḍi azhud uruka
verumai nīṅkuṁ vāzhvilē nārāyaṇā
namō nārāyaṇā namō nārāyaṇā
namō nārāyaṇā

As name and fame delude you, and words of praise weaken you, you need dispassion to keep the mind on an even keel. Through singing and dancing with tearful eyes, wants will disappear from your life. Narayana namo narayana.

seyvatellāṁ tānenḍru
jīvan garvvaṁ koḷḷavē
kīzhē vizhuṁ pōtutānē
dēvan pādaṁ tēḍumē
karaṁ pattri karai sēra
nāḷuṁ ēṅki solluvōṁ nārāyaṇā
namō nārāyaṇā namō nārāyaṇā
namō nārāyaṇā

As the proud ego proclaims its doership, only upon a hard fall will you seek the Lord's feet. To reach ashore from the cycle of birth and death, let us cry out His name.

KĀNĀTA MĀJHĒ (MARATHI)

kānāta mājhē gūjata āhē
jay jay viṭhala nāma tujhē
manāta mājhyā virājita āhē
panḍharī nāthā rūp tujhē

Your divine name, Vithala, is ringing in my ears; Your divine form is shining in my mind.

Bhaktichyā laharīt vāhūna gēlī
jagāchī rūchī mājhyā manī
pāuna tujhyā nāmāchē dhana mī
jhālō yā jagāta sārvāñ dhanī

In a wave of devotion for You my interest in this world has been washed away. When I gained the wealth of Your name I became the owner of everything in this world.

Kōṇāśī krōdh karū mī dēvā
tuch disē malā sarvāta rē
nirmala prēmala kasā mī jhālō
tujhyā kṛpē chā chamatkāra rē

I see You in everybody; how can I then show anger to anyone, O Lord? How is it that I became purified and compassionate? That is the miracle of Your grace.

KANDARPPAKŌṬI SUNDARĀ (TELUGU)

kandarppakōṭi sundarā
mandaragiri śūradharā
vanamāli nagadharā
jagadīśvarā bhavabhayahara kēśavā

God who is infinitely beautiful and extremely capable, who lifted Mandhara mountain, who wears the garland of wild flowers around His neck. Lord of the world, who removes the fear of the world.

kēśavā jay mādhavā gōpikā
vallabhā madhusūdanā muraharā

Glory to Madhava, beloved of the gopis, the one who killed the demon Mura.

kamalākṣa laṣmīpati
vāsudēva nārāyaṇa
śrīdharā bhudharā
puruṣōttamā karuṇākarā kēśvā

Lotus-eyed one, consort of Goddess Lakshmi. Son of Vasudeva, Lord of the world. The one who supports Lakshmi (wealth) and who supports the earth. You are the best among men, O compassionate Keshava!

nanduni varasuta
sumanōhara suguṇākarā
dvārakā purapālakā
puruṣōttamā karuṇākarā kēśavā

Blessed child of Nanda, beautiful one, embodiment of all good qualities, ruler of Dwaraka. You are the best among men, O compassionate Keshava!

bhadrārchita śrīcaraṇā
śaraṇamu sarvēśvarā
śamkhacakra maṇidharā
puruṣōttamā karuṇākarā kēśvā

O Lord of All, I surrender to Your auspicious feet that bestow protection for those who worship them. You wear the jewel, conch, and disc. You are the best among men, O compassionate Keshava!

KANIVOṬUKĀTTARUḶĪṬAṆAMĒ

(MALAYALAM)

kanivoṭukāttaruḷīṭaṇamē, mama
mati kaluṣatakaḷ akattaṇamē
aṭimalar tozhutiṭum aṭiyane viravoṭu
kaṭa mizhiyāl onnuzhiyaṇamē

Please be kind, protect and bless me, remove the confusion (dirt) in my mind. Please look upon me with kind eyes, this humble one prostrating at Your feet.

kadanakkaṭalala nīntivarunnōr –
kkabhayam tavatirukazhalaṭikaḷ
karuṇayilorutari taraṇē, mama mati
timirindhataviṭṭu ṇarviyalān!

Your feet are the only refuge for those swimming in the ocean of sorrow. Please lend me at least a grain of Your compassion, so my mind may escape from darkness and attain light.

itaḷitaḷāyennakamalar viriyum
śubhadinam āgatamākaṇamē
karaḷalivārnna jaganmayi, tavatiru
karalāḷanagati yēkaṇamē!

Let this be the auspicious day when my mind's petals blossom! O Mother of the world, illuminate the path to bliss!

KAṆṆANDE MĀRILE (MALAYALAM)

kaṇṇande mārile vanamālayākuvān
kaṇṇande kālil poncilambukaḷākuvān
kaṇṇande kaiyile muraḷikayākuvān
kaṇṇande puñciri pālnukarnnīṭuvān
entu ñān ceyyeṇṭū?
entu ñān ceyyeṇṭū?

What can I do? What can I do? How can I become the garland of wildflowers on Krishna's chest? How can I become the anklets that jingle on Krishna's feet? How can I become the flute in Krishna's hands? How can I enjoy the nectar of Krishna's smile?

kaṇṇande pāṭṭukaḷ pāṭi naṭakkuvān
kaṇṇande pāṭṭinu tāḷamiṭṭāṭuvān
entu ñān ceyyēṇṭū?
entu ñān ceyyēṇṭū?

What can I do? What can I do? How can I lose myself singing Krishna's glory? How can I dance to the rhythm of Krishna's tune?

ennumennum ende kaṇṇanāyiīṭuvān
ennile ninne ñān ennum ariyuvān
entu ñān ceyyēṇṭū
entu ñān ceyyēṇṭū

What can I do? What can I do? How can I become one with Krishna for eternity, realize Him, see Him always in my mind?

kaṇṇane ennennum kaṇḍurasikkuvān
kaṇṇande cintakaḷ mātramāyīṭuvān
entu ñān ceyyēṇṭū
entu ñān ceyyēṇṭū

What can I do? What can I do? How can I ceaselessly visualize His beautiful form, immersed in His bliss, with thoughts of Him reverberating in my mind like sacred mantras?

KAṆṆE IMAI KĀPPATUPŌL (TAMIL)

kaṇṇe imai kāppatupōl
maṇṇe maram kāppatupōl
nammeyellām kāttiṭuvāy – māriyamma
nam kavalaiyellām pōkkiḍuvāḷ māriyamma

As the eyelid protects the eye, as the soil protects the tree, so should You take care of all of us, Mariyamma. Remove all our sorrows!

kaṇṇukkūḷḷē kaṇṇāga
neṇcukkuḷḷē neṇcāga
uḷḷukkuḷḷē uraintiḍuvāḷ māriyamma – itai
uṇarumbōtu veḷippaḍuvāḷ – māriyamma

Be as the eye of the eye, the heart of the heart. Oh Mariyamma, reside in me. When I realize this truth, Mariyamma will reveal Herself!

tan nalattai marantuviṭṭu
dharaṇikkāga vāzhukindra
ponmanattai virūmbiḍuvāḷ māriyammā – atai
pūvaipōla cūṭiḍuvāḷ - māriyamma

She is fond of the hearts of those who forget themselves and live for others; Mariyamma adorns Herself with such hearts as if they were flowers.

tannaippola aḍuttavarai
kāṇamuyalum manitarūkku
tattuvamāy viḷankiḍuvāḷ māriyamma - parama
sattiyattai uṇarttiṭuvāḷ – māriyamma

To those who try to see others as themselves, She shines as the essence of the supreme truth, and makes them awaken to that truth.

KAṆṆIMAYKĀTE (MALAYALAM)

kaṇṇimaykāte annum
kālocha yōrttu rādha
kaṇṇane kānanattil
kāttirunnu

Radha awaited the arrival of Krishna in the forest. She would not close Her eyes even for a moment. Her mind dwelled incessantly on the smallest movements of Krishna's feet.

ētō viṣāda maunam
kallichurañña pōle
tāraka kaṇmalarum
vāṭininnu (2x)

Radha's eyes, resembling stars, began to wilt like flowers. A sorrowful silence descended like a heavy stone.

kaṇṇan varāññatōrtta
tiṇṇam piṭaññu rādha
tīkanalāzhiyil kāl
āzhnnapōle (2x)

As Radha began to suspect that Krishna might not come She suffered as if Her feet had been dipped in a sea of fire.

ārōvarunna pōle
dūre nizhalanakam
rādha piṭaññeṇīttu
pāravaśyam (2x)

Far away a shadow moved as if someone was coming. Radha quickly rose up in eagerness.

pēlavāmgam tarichu
pīlinētram mizhichu
śvāsatālam nilachu
nōkininnu (2x)

As She stared into the distance Her breathing became constricted and Her eyes, resembling peacock feathers, became still. Her soft body became stiff.

kālchilambocha kēlke
kāttētta pūvupōle
ātma harṣōn mādattā
lāṭi rādha (2x)

As She heard the soft sound of anklets She danced in bliss like a flower moving in a breeze.

rādhē varū vari ken
ētō svarānu bhūti

pūntēnurava pōle
vārnnozhuki (2x)

She heard a sound, "oh Radha, come closer," which flowed as if from the source of a river of nectar.

KAṆṆIRĀL KAṆṆĀ (MALAYALAM)

kaṇṇirāl kaṇṇā! kalarnnuninnīṭunno-
rōrmmakaḷ ninne valamvechozhuki
allum pakalum paravaśamākkume-
nnuḷḷam nirāśayilāzhān viṭolle

My memories of You, mixed with tears, flow constantly around my mind, make me dizzy day and night. Please do not let my mind drown in hopelessness.

nī marannīṭilum ñān marannīṭumō
ī muḷantaṇḍindeyīṇam
kāvalāyeppōzhum ñānirunnīṭumboḷ
dūrasthanallennu tōnnum – kaṇṇan
bāhyasthanallennu tonnum

Even if You forget, will I ever forget the tune of this flute? Kanna! You don't appear to be far away. You don't seem like a stranger.

entō marannuvechennapolannu nī
cintichu mandam kaṭannupoyi
prāṇanō? pāzhmuḷantaṇḍō? maravicha
cintayil cāri ñān ninnupōyi

You walked away slowly, as if You were forgetting something. Was it my life breath that You forgot, or the bamboo flute? I stood there, frozen in thought.

annuṭoṭṭinnōḷam kaṇṇan kaḷavēṇu
ūtiyiṭṭillennu kēṭṭu
enkilum kēḷkkāmenikkā manōjñāmam
sangītadhārayonninnum

I heard that since that day, Kanna has not played His flute, but I still hear that flow of music in my mind.

KARAYALLĒ PAITALE (MALAYALAM)

karayallē paitalē karayallē paitalē
tārāṭṭu pāṭuvān ammayillē
sandigdham mākumen antarāḷattilum
sangītamēkuvān ammayillē ammayillē

Don't cry, little one, don't cry - isn't Mother here to sing a lullaby? In my confused mind, isn't Mother here to bestow the music?

nanayallē mizhikaḷe nanayallē mizhikaḷe
kaṇṇīr tuṭaykkuvān ammayillē
śōkamī jīvita pātayilennennum
āśvāsamēkuvān ammayillē ammayillē

Eyes, do not become wet- isn't Mother here to dry your tears? In this sorrowful path of life, isn't Mother always there to console you?

taḷaralē paitalē taḷaralē paitalē
kūṭe naṭakkuvān ammayillē
iṭarunna jīvitapātayilennennum
vazhikāṭṭiyākuvān ammayillē ammayillē

Little one, do not become tired, do not be weary. Isn't Mother walking alongside you? In this faltering path of life, isn't Mother always there to show the way?

KARAYĀTTA KAṆṆANIN (MALAYALAM)

kaṇṇā, kaṇṇā, kaṇṇā
karayātta kaṇṇaninnentē – en
karayunna kaṇṇinōṭiṣṭam
kadanaṅaḷillātta kaṇṇā – enne
karayikkum virahamakattū - kaṇṇā

O Krishna who never cries, why are my crying eyes so dear to You? O Krishna, who is immune to sorrow, please remove the separation from You that makes me weep.

puzhayōḷam mizhinīrozhukkī - ñān
tuzhayunnu virahattin tōṇi
azhal kāttil en nauka kaṇṇā
cuzhiyil peṭṭāzhnnu pōkunnu - kaṇṇā

In this flood of tears that flows like a river, I row the boat of separation; O Krishna! Prey to the winds of grief, my boat is caught in a whirlpool and is sinking fast!

kozhiyunnen prēmaprasūnam
azhiyunnu tazhukalillāte
puzhuvinnirayākum munnē – nī
tazhukiyaṇarttīṭū kaṇṇā

Without an embrace from You, my love may fall away and disappear. Before I become the food of worms, please embrace and save me, O Krishna!

KARM KI NADIYĀ (HINDI)

karm ki nadiyā bahati jāyē
karm ki nadiyā bahati jāyē

The river of destiny keeps flowing.

kōyi iski gati nahi jānē
kōyi na iskā sat pahcānē
kōn himālaya janmē iskō
kis sāgar mē khul mil jāyē

Nobody knows its condition nor its truth. Which Himalaya it was born from or which ocean it merges with is unknown.

ujlē mēlē sab jal ismē
tṛpti ismē sab chal ismē
kōyi pīvē ghātak viṣ hi
kōyi amrit ras hi pāvē

Both clean and dirty waters merge in it. It is full of both contentment and discontentment. Some drink it as poison, others drink it as nectar.

karmaṇ bhōgi sab kā man hi
naṣṭh na hōtā kōyi kaṇ bhi
kāl anantā kī ghaṭhiyō mē
ik tan āyē ik tan jāyē

The human mind enjoys material gratification. It is always preoccupied with fulfilling its selfish desires. As a result, the cycle of human birth and death continues. The soul leaves the body and takes birth in another human form. It never attains salvation.

tam mē ḍūbē yugal kinārē
sīmit jin mē sukh dukh sārē
kōyi mar kar lauṭ na pāyā
jō kōyi ākar bēdh batāyē

Human beings are drowned in darkness. They are so limited to their own happiness and suffering. After leaving this world, they do not come back to share moments of suffering with others.

KARUMAIYILĒ (TAMIL)

karumaiyilē putumai kaṇṭēn kāḷī - untan
kaṇkaḷilē kanivu kaṇṭēn dēvī
perumaiyinai pāṭiṭavē kāḷī - sollin
varumaiyilē vāṭi ninṭrēn dēvī
kāḷiyamma durgā dēviyamma

O Kali! In the blackness of Your hue, I saw newness. In Your eyes, I saw compassion. O Devi, I have no words to describe Your greatness. O Mother Kali, divine Mother Durga!

karuvaraiyil unaturuvam kaṇṭēn - daiva
tiruvazhakil manamuruki ninṭrēn
varuvatōṭ cenṭrarellām nīnki - nikazhum
oru gaṇattil vāzhum pēr koṇṭēn
kāḷiyamma durgā dēviyamma

I came to the sanctum, and Your beauty melted my heart. Leaving past and future behind, I have the fortune to live in the present. O Mother Kali, divine Mother Durga!

irumaiyilē kāṇumpōt nānum - untan
aṭimai enṭrē perumaiyōṭ vāzhvēn
orumaiyilē onṭrum pōt nāmum - āzha
kaṭalum atan alaiyum pōla vanṭrō
kāḷiyamma durgā deviyamma

Seeing the dual aspect, I will become Your slave. In the advaita aspect (oneness), like the wave and the sea, will You and I become one? O Mother Kali, divine Mother Durga!

KARUṆĀSĀGARĀ (TAMIL)

karuṇāsāgarā śrīrāmā
pāvananāma param dhāma
śrīrāmā enkaḷ rājā rāmā
mohana rāmā raghurāmā

Ocean of compassion, Sri Rama, pure name, supreme abode. Sri Rama, our king Rama, beautiful Rama of the Raghu clan!

uḷḷam uruki uṇarvin uṇarvai
uḷḷattil uṇara vaippāyo
veḷḷam pōndra unatanpil
vēṇḍi uraiya vaippāyo

Will You make me realize, my heart melting, that You are closer than the closest? Your love equals pure sweetness. Make me understand the sweetness of Your love.

kāṇum kāṭci kānal nīr ena
karuttinil uṇara vaippāyo
niraimatiyāy en uḷḷam atil
oḷiyin uruvāy oḷirvāyo

Everything I see is a mirage. won't You make me realize that? Won't You shine inside my heart like the full moon?

rāmā śrīrāmā rāmā param dhāmā
rāmā raghurāmā rāmā jayarāmā

O Lord Rama, Supreme Abode! Victory to You, O Rama!

KĒVĀ BHĀVAMĀ (GUJARATI)

kēvā bhāvamā mā tū āvē
kyā rūpa mā tū āvē
jyārē jyārē tanē pōkārū
tū mārī sāthē nē sāthē

O Mother, You come before me in an exalted state. How many forms does my Mother assume? Whenever I call You, Mother, I find that You are with me.

hū jō visārū mā
tū manē nā visārē
sukh mā hū tānē bhūlū chattā
dukh mā tū mārī pāsē

Even if I forget You, Mother, I know that You will never forget me. If I forget You in my happiness, You will still be beside me in my sorrow.

man mā rahē tārō vās
vinatī mārī sūnō āj
bhūl hū karū jyārē kōyī
ṭōkajē tū man tyārē

Accept this request of mine and make my mind Your abode. Whenever I do something wrong, Mother, point it out to me then and there.

KHŌL DARVĀZĀ (PUNJABI)

khōl darvāzā śērā vāliyēnī
mahā ṛānīyēnī - dē darśanjvālā
kardē pagat pukār japaṇ tērē nāṁ – dī mālā
khōl darvāsā śērāvāliyē

O Devi who rides the lion, O Great Queen, please open the door to Your temple. We, all Your devotees, are calling You, constantly chanting Your name. O Mother, please open the door!

dvārē tērēnī maiyā sangatā he āyiyānī ambē
sangtā he āyiyā
tērē pahāḍādiyā caḍhkē caḍhāyiyānī ambē
caḍhkē caḍhāyiyā
pēṭhā lēyāyē tērē dvār mā
dēdī dār mā mē ōganhārī
dar tērē āḍiggīmē pāpanhārī

O Mother, all the devotees have come to Your door. We have climbed the mountain to bring You our gifts. O Mother, we aspirants have come to You; please accept our offerings!

tērī gūphādī maiyā śān nirālīnī ambē
śān nirālī
sidd vicch vassēsūyē cōlēyā vālīnī ambē
cōlēyā vālī
hōkē simh savār mā –
dēdī dār mā – assī bacchḍē tērē
pāvēha pūt – kapūtā tē tērē

O Mother, who lives in a beautiful cave, You are the one who bestows Her boons on all Her devotees. O Mother, ride Your lion; please bless us with Your vision. We stand at Your door, awaiting Your darshan. You accept whoever seeks Your grace, whether he be noble or sinful: You turn no one away.

dvāre tērē jēḍā āyā savālīnī ambē
āyā savālī
mangiyā murādā pāvē jāyē nā khālīnī ambē
jāyē nā khālī
sadāravā tērē nāl mā –
ehō ās mā – tērē gun gāvā mē
tērē sōnē darbārttē mē āvā

I have come to Your golden temple. O Mother, my only desire is to be with You and sing Your glories at every moment.

jay mātā dī jay mātā dī

May I always sing, "Victory to the divine Mother!"

KISKĪ KHŌJ (HINDI)

kiskī khōj mē tu bandē
dinrāt hai bētāb
chain jō ḍhunḍe jag mē tu
vō andar tērē vās

O man, day and night, whom are you searching for? The peace you are trying to find is already dwelling in your heart.

mīn ramē jō sāgar mē
gar lāgē uskō pyās
tērī daśā bhī bhinn nahī
rang nahī tu hē rājā

O man, you are not a beggar but a king! Your condition is similar to that of a fish always thirsty though surrounded in water.

sant mahān jitnē āyē
ānand kā mārgg batāyē
mōh rāg kō kār dē tyāg
karnā prabhu sē anurāg

Many realized souls have come and shown the path of happiness and joy. Give up all your desires and attachments and bind yourself to the Lord.

jāg jāg tu nidrā sē
lakśya kō kar sākār
mānava janma pānē kā avasar
āyē na bār bār

O man, wake up, wake up from deep sleep. Realize your goals. The good fortune of a human birth does not come again and again!

KŌTHĀ TUMĪ JONANĪ (BENGALI)

kōthā tumī jonanī
jonanī jonanī
etō ḍāki tobū dāo nā śāṭā
kōthā tumī jonanī

Mother, where are You? O Mother, O Mother! I call out to You so often but still You don't respond!

kāḷi mā kāḷi mā kāḷi mā
kāḷi mā kāḷi mā kāḷi mā kaḷi mā

O Mother, Mother Kali!

phiriteci anāth jībon pathē
jag jananīr cēle pather dhulātē

kēmon mā ēr jigāśe śobē
bolō magōki uttar dēbē

I wander like an orphan on the path of life. Universal Mother's child on the dusty road. Everyone wonders, 'What kind of a mother does he have?' Tell me Mother, what reply will You give them?

harānō sṛti paṭe jē monē
chilām tabkōlē kōn jonomē

I recall a lost memory of being in Your lap in a previous birth.

dayā karō tumī karuṇa pāthār
kōlē nāvo tūlē jonani āmār
snēha śuddha śikt karō tumi mōre
bēddhē rākhō mōrētab bāhuḍōre

Have mercy, oh ocean of compassion! My Mother, take me into Your lap. Shower me with pure motherly love, keep me in Your embrace!

KṚṢṆA GŌVINDA GŌPĀLA (HINDI)

kṛṣṇa gōvinda gōpāla rām harī nām gāvō
gōpāla nāchō nāchō hamrē sang

Sing the Lord's names Krishna, Govinda, Gopala, Ram, Hari! O Krishna, please dance with us!

ānā kānhā tū hamrē pās
nāch nachyyō tū hamrē sāth
tērī muralī kē gān sang nāch karē
nāch nāch kē sāth gān karē
kānhā ō kṛṣṇa gōvinda

Please come to us Krishna and dance in our company! We dance to the song of Your flute. Dancing, we sing with You! Krishna, O Krishna!

sundar sundar tū kitnā sundar
mana mōhan tū dil kē andar
tērī mahimā hē sabsē pār
tērī līlā hē sabsē dhār

O how beautiful You are! You are so captivating! Your glory is beyond all. Your sport is beyond all?

KṚṢṆĀ NINNĀ BĀLA LĪLE (KANNADA)

kṛṣṇa nanna kṛṣṇā!
bālakṛṣṇa bāla kṛṣṇā!

O Krishna, my Krishna, O little Krishna!

kṛṣṇā ninnā bāla līle
kaṇṇi geṣṭānanda
ninna jōḍi āṭuvudēnō
ānanda apāra

O Krishna, how pleasing are Your childhood games. Playing with You brings me immense joy.

kṛṣṇā bālakṛṣṇā
nīla kṛṣṇā nanna kṛṣṇā

O Krishna, O little Krishna, O blue Krishna, O my Krishna!

nīli tāvare mogadali miñcide
beṇṇe kaḷḷana nōṭṭa
edeyali eddide prēma pūra
hebbale ārbhaṭā

The butter thief's sidelong glances flash in His blue lotus face. A flood of love rises in my heart, the rumbling of huge tidal waves.

giridhara ninna kiruberaḷāṭa
muraḷī gānavō
munkurulāṭa gōpiraka hṛdayadī
prēma sañcārā

O He who lifted the mountain, the play of Your little finger creates tunes on the flute. The play of Your curls inspires reverberations of love in the hearts of the gopis.

kinkiṇi kilikili nūpura jaṇajaṇa
sṛṣṭi spandanā
muttina adhara sparśadi nīṭu
viśvadarśanā

The jingling of the ornaments around Your waist and Your ankles are truly the vibrations of creation. Grant me the universal vision with the touch of Your lips in a kiss.

KURIYANI KAṆṆĪRU (TELUGU)

kuriyani kaṇṇīru pannīrugā tallī
nī pāda padmamula śaraṇupondi

Let my tears flow as perfumed water finding refuge at Your lotus feet.

viriyani ārtthine virimālagā māri
nī charaṇayugalipai paravasiññchi

Let my unfulfilled desires blossom as flower garlands at Your lotus feet.

palukani pilupune praṇava nādamu rīti
nī laḷita padamulanu yadanu nilipi

Let my unspoken words resonate like Om, and establish Your soft feet in my heart.

karugani ahamune karppūrahāratai
nī amṛta mūrttini hṛdini kolichi

Let my unmelting ego disintegrate as camphor in worship of Your divine form in my heart.

panḍanī nā bratuku guṇḍelōtula nīvu
kōṭi sūryula prabhala koluvu tīri

Let my life attain fruition with You shining in the depths of my heart with the brilliance of a thousand suns.

KURUMBUKKĀRA (TAMIL)

kurumbukkāra kaṇṇan līlai kēṭka kēṭka inikkumē
karumbu pōla inikkum atai ninaikka uḷḷam makizhumē
arumai mukham kāṇachentrāl kaṭamaikkuppō embān
kaṭamayilē mūzhkiviṭṭāl marandanaiyō embān kurumbukkārā

Kanna, O mischievous one, hearing about Your divine play brings me more and more joy. Contemplating Your divine play, sweet as sugarcane, gladdens my heart. When we come closer to look at His beautiful face, He bids us to our work (duty). When we become immersed in work, He says we have forgotten Him. O mischievous one.

toṭṭuppēsa oṭṭinintrāl taṭṭiviṭṭu selvān
eṭṭanirkkum gōpiyarai kiṭṭacentraṇaippān
maṭṭam taṭṭi piraretiril kēli seytu makizhvān
tiṭṭam pōṭṭu namataiyellām tiruṭichentru maraivān
tiruṭichentru maraivān

If we sidle up to Him, He pushes us away, goes to the gopi standing far away, and hugs her. He takes delight in poking fun at us. He schemes to steal everything that belongs to us, and then hides Himself.

tanakketuvum teriyātena mandiram pōl solvān
vāyu tirandāl aṇḍāmellām namakkutteriya seyvān
tanakketuvum vēṇḍāmena eppozhutum solvān
uṭal poruḷōṭāviyellām sontamākki koḷvān
sontamākki koḷvān

He repeatedly says that He knows nothing, but when He opens His mouth, He reveals the whole universe. He says always that He needs nothing; He captures us, heart and soul.

gōpiyarin mannavanai gōpālabāla
rādhaikkoru mādhavanē rādhāvilōlā

O cowherd boy, Lord of the gopis. O consort of Radha, Her joy and delight.

LĪLĀ ADDHUTA DIVYA CHARITA TAVA (MARATHI)

līlā addhuta divya charita tava
pāhūnī hī vṛttī ramalī
ambikē śaraṇ mī padayūgalī (2)

Your divine play is wonderful; Your life is divine. Seeing it, the modifications of the mind subside. O divine Mother, we take refuge at Your lotus feet.

bhav sāgar yā buḍatā būḍatā
sāvariḷē tū dharūnī hātā
kṛtañja tēchē āsū jharatī
hōtā tava bhēṭī hōtā tava bhēṭī
-- ōmātā hōtā tava bhēṭī

I was drowning in this ocean of samsara [cycle of birth and death] but You saved me by holding my hand. Tears of gratitude started flowing when I met You.

ēka māgaṇē ambē ātā
antim kṣaṇi tū adharī vastā
kṛtārtha hōyil jīvana mājhē
asatā tū zhavaḷī asatā tū zhavaḷī
-- ōmātā asatā tū zhavaḷī

O Mother, give me one boon now. May Your holy name be ever on my lips until my last breath. If You be with me in my last moment, my life will be blessed.

MĀ ILAVĒLUPU (TELUGU)

mā ilavēlupu nīvē kadammā
karuṇatō mammū kāpāḍammā

You are our family deity; O Mother, protect us with your compassion.

nī ārādhana vidhamē telipi
mā pūjalanē saphalamu cēsi
nī sannidhinē niratamu nilipi
mā manasulanē bāguga cēsina

You teach us how to worship; make our prayers successful. Fix Your presence here eternally; make our minds pure.

ammā varadāyinī bhakta paripālini
janma phaladāyinī jaya bhavatārini

O Mother who grants boons and protects the devotees! You grant the fruit of life and carry us across the ocean of samsara!

nī kanusannala nīḍana bratukē
hāyigā ōlalē āḍutu sāgē
nī padamulanē cittamunantu
talacēnu kolicēnu ēnāṭiki

In the shade of Your loving glance, life passes happily in play. We remember You, and worship Your holy feet forever.

MĀ JAY JAY MĀ (HINDI)

mā jay mā jay jay mā
jay jay mā jay jay mā jay mā jay mā

Victory to Mother!

mā darśan dē
tū he jagadīśvarī
mamatāmayi paramēśvarī

Give me darshan, O Mother of the universe, compassionate, supreme Goddess.

hṛdayēśvarī tū he bhayahāriṇī
varadāyinī bhavatāriṇī

You reside in the heart, and alleviate all fears. You bestow boons and take us across the ocean of life.

tū dil mē ākē bas jānā mā
haskē cāndni barsānā mā

Come and dwell in my heart, Mother. Smile and shower us with moonlight, Mother.

bhīgē tanman śītal hō mā
mērā jīvan dhanya bane mā

O Mother, cool the heat of this worldly life and make this human birth worthwhile.

karuṇā sē mujhe
nehalānā mā
man kā jalan miṭā dēnā mā

Bathe me with Your compassion, Mother, and rid me of the burning of my heart.

simirū har pal tujh
kō hī mā
ēsā var mujhe dēnā maiyā

Bless me that I may think of You every moment, O Mother.

MAKARANDA MĀDHURYA (TELUGU)

makaranda mādhurya muna - tēnlēnduku
malletōṭṭa chērenu bhramaramu
ā prēma mādhuryamuna tēlēnduku - amma
oḍiki chērēnu nāmanam - ēdi
bhramaramā telusukō madhuramu

The honey bee goes to the jasmine garden to enjoy the sweetness of nectar. My mind goes to Amma's lap to enjoy the sweetness of that Divine Love. O honey bee, know which is sweeter.

Tīrani dāhamunu tīrcchuku nēnduku
Mēghamukai chātakamu vēcchenu
ā kṛpāvarṣamuna taḍisēnduku - amma
chūpukai vēchēnu nāmanam - chātakamā
dēnitō dāhamu tīrunō

The chataka bird waits for rain clouds in quench its unquenchable thirst. My mind waits for Amma's glance to get drenched in the rain of Her grace. O Chataka, know what quenches the thirst.

Nirmala jalālalō vihariñchēnduku
Himasarasu rāyañcha chērenu
ānandavīchikala vihariñchēnduku - amma
pādamu chērenu nāmanam - ānandamu
rāyañcha endulo

The royal swan goes to the Mana sarovar to enjoy the swim in pure waters. My mind goes to Amma's feet to swim in the waves of bliss. In what does bliss lie - O royal swan?

MANAMENḌRUM UNDAN VĪDU

(TAMIL)

manamenḍrum undan vīdu
marundu enḍrum untiru nīru
idamāna mozhikalai kūru
iduvandro perum pēru

My mind is ever Your abode. Your sacred ash is the medicine. Is it not my good fortune to listen to Your soothing words?

anpāi nī kaḍaikan pārtu
arulāl enai karayil sērtu
vemmāya piṇitanai tīrtu
vidi tannai nalamāy māṭru

Give me a loving glance. With Your grace, take me across the water. Remove the disease of illusion. Change my fate to goodness.

eduvellām enakiḍayūr
adan kūṭrāy aran nī māru
nīyinḍri gatiyār vēru
nī tāne kanivin mēru

You change the aspect of whatever obstacle comes to me. Without You there is no refuge. You are the mountain of compassion.

hara hara hara hara shankara
shiva shiva shiva shiva sada shiva
shambho shankara sarvesha
sharanam sharanam samba shiva

MANASSIL NĪLA SARASIL (MALAYALAM)

manassil nīla sarasil
oru sarasīrūham viriññu
azhakil bhāva niravil
oru sarasijānanam teḷiññu!

In the stillness of my mind, a beautiful lotus bloomed. In the beauty of that flower, I saw Your enchanting face.

amaratvakānti vitarunna – jñāna
varadāna rūpavadanam
teḷivuttu kaṇḍu nirabhakti pūṇḍu
nanavārnniṭunna nayanam

When I saw Your everlasting beauty, devotion welled up inside of me, and I began to cry.

akaneññu nīri asidhāra-yāya
vazhi-yetra tāṇḍi-yoṭuvil
abhivandyarāya ṛṣivṛndamātma
mizhiyālariñña poruḷ, nī

After so much desperate searching, all the great sages came to know You through the inner Self.

MANGAḶA NĀYAKI (TAMIL)

mangaḷa nāyaki ādiparāśakti
mangaḷam ponkavīttriruntāḷ
marakata uru mayil naṭai azhakil
yāzhisaiyuṭan iyarkaiyin ezhilil
innisaiyōṭu narttanamāṭi
mandiram mozhintu neñcam pukuntāḷ

O Adiparashakti, the auspicious one is seated auspiciously on Her throne. Her form shines like a diamond, Her gait is like that of a peacock. Accompanied by the sound of the divine veena and the beauty of nature, She comes into my heart, chanting a mantra.

nadiyōram kuḷirtēntral inimai
maṇamiraikka malarvanam atilāṭum
mayilāṭa kuyil kūvum kārmēgham
malarmaṇḍapattil alankāram koṇḍāṭṭam
tiruvizhā

A cool breeze can be felt on the banks of the river. The flower garden, exuding a sweet fragrance, dances to its tune. The dancing peacock is a blissful sight to behold, along with the singing bird. The hall is decorated grandly, as if for a festival.

kalaikaṇkaḷ naṭanam puriyum
tiruviḷakkin oḷisintum sānnidhyam
pūmālai tōraṇangaḷ āṭivarum
meymarantu kāṇbōrkku daivīkadarśanam

Devi's beautiful eyes move about as if dancing. The divine lamp spreads the light of peace and tranquility; it's flame sways to and fro. Forgetting themselves, those who witness it enjoy the divine vision.

jay jay gāyatri śrīvidyai śankari
jay jay jñānasvarūpiṇi vāṇi
jay jay vēdanāyaki vittaki
jay jay cāmuṇḍēśvari māyi

Glory to Gayatri, Sri Vidya and Shankari! Hail to Sarasvati, the Goddess of knowledge! Glory to She who leads the Vedas, victory to the slayer of Chanda and Munda!

MĀ O MĀ (GUJARATI)

mā o mā mārī mā
tārā sivā kōṇ mārū
tārā sivā mane
nā jōve kōyī bījū

Mother, I have no one other than You. I also don't want anyone besides You.

tu mārī sāthī tu sangāthī
tu mārā śvāsōnā śvāsō śvās
rōm rōm mā tārō vās
kyārē samāviś mujnē tuj mā

You are my friend, You are my companion, You dwell in each breath I take; when will You merge me in You?

tu mārī pāsē chatā hun tārāthī dūr
tāru māru kēvu ā bandhan
hu ātmā tun paramātmā
kyārē samāviś mujne tuj mā

What sort of relationship is this? You are always by my side, yet I am so far from You. I am the atma (self), You are paramatma (supreme Self); when will You merge me in You?

tu mārī dēvī ā jagnī tu jananī
tārā caraṇoma cārō lōk
hu ā jagmā ā jag tuj mā
kyārē samāviś mujnē tuj mā
mā ō mā

You are my Devi, You are the mother of this world, the four worlds are at Your feet. I am of this world, and this world remains in You; when will You merge me in You?

MĒRĀ MUJH MAIN (PUNJABI)

mērā mujh main kuch nahi maiyyā
jō kuch hai ō tū hī maiyyā
tērā tujhkō saupkkē maiyyā
mēri maiyyā ō mēri maiyā main
tērē vich racadā jāvā mē jay mātādi gāvā

I have nothing in me that is mine, All that I have belongs to You. May I surrender everything to You that is Yours and merge in You.

jithē dekhā tūhī dissdā, har dil dē vich tūhi
tēri ḍōr vich har dil nū mai, ek dil kardā jāvā
sukh vī tērā dukh vī tērā, sab racanā hai teri maiyā
tērā tērā kardā hī mai, tērē vich racadā jāvā – main
tērē vich racadā jāvā

Wherever I look, I see only You; You are in every heart. May we join all hearts together with the thread that leads to Your heart. Happiness, sorrow, the entire creation is Yours. May we see everything as Your grace and merge in You.

śērāvāli jōttāvāli lāṭhāvāli
mehrāvāli pahadavāli polipāli maiya
tērē vich racadā jāvā, mē jay mātādi gāvā

kar kirpā kī isa sēvakkdī ichā hūvē pūri
mangā nā kuch tērē tō mai
dhan dhan kardā jāvā
kehendē sadguru kaḷḷā nahi tū
tēynū pal pal cukkdā jāvā

ik kadamu tū mērēval cukkdā dassa kadama
mai āvā
dassa kadamu mē āvā

Bestow Your blessings on this servant so that his desire is fulfilled; I don't ask for anything but just want to thank You. The Satguru says, "You are not alone in this world, I am always carrying You along. When You take one step towards Me, I take ten steps towards You."

gajj ke gāvō, jay mātādi
phatē bulāvō, jay mātādi
mai nahi suṇēyā, jay mātādi
ral mil gāvō, jay mātādi

Sing with all your might. Victory to Mother! Call out for victory. Victory to Mother! Sing louder, I can't hear you. Victory to Mother! Let us all sing together. Victory to Mother!

MĀ TĒRĒ CARAṆŌ MĒ JŌ (HINDI)

mā tērē caraṇō mē jō
ātē hē sīs jhukātē
unkō tū apnātī hai
sab-vānchit vara dētī hai

Mother You accept as Your own those who bow down at Your feet and bestow upon them the boons they seek.

mā ambē maiyā jananī
mātā hai tū duniyā kī
bhavsāgar naiyā tūhai
ham kō tū pārlagāde

O Mother! You are Mother to the whole world. You are the boat that ferries one across the river of transmigration. Ferry us across!

ab dērī mat karnā mā
bālak mai bichuḍā tujhsē
tūhī ab hāth baḍhākē
mujhkō majhdhār se bacādē

Now please don't delay further, I'm just a child separated from You. Please extend Your hand and save me, I'm drowning midstream.

mē tērē pāv paḍāhūn
karuṇā sē rāh dikhā dē
andhiyārā phail raha hē
jaldī tū ghar pahuṅcā dē

I am lying at Your feet, be compassionate and show me the way. Darkness is spreading all around. Quickly! carry me home.

mā tū hē jīvan tārā
sankaṭmē tūhi sāhārā
tū yād kabhī kar mērē
jīvan mē hō ujiyārā

Mother You are the life, You are the help in difficult times. Please think of me too, so the light enters my life.

jai jagagambe jai jagadambe
jai jagadambe jai jagadambe
jai jagagambe jai jagadambe
jai jagadambe jai jagadambe

Victory to the Mother of the universe!

MALAIMAKAḶĒ TĀYĒ (TAMIL)

malaimakaḷē tāyē maunamum mārātō
marukiṭum makanivanin mayakkam tīrātō

O Mother! Daughter of the Mountain (Himavan), please don't keep silent. Won't You alleviate the suffering of Your tormented son?

māyai ena ulakai maraikaḷ ōdidinum
manatil piṭipaṭṭēn matiyum mayankukirēn
marakata māmaṇiyē mankaḷa oḷi vaṭivē
manakkōyil tanil vara tāmatam ēnō?

I run around blindly in this illusory world. My mind is caught in Maya, and my brain feels dizzy. O shining divine jewel! Why do You wait to come and live in my heart?

kōṭiporuḷ vēṇḍēn peyarōṭu pukazh vēṇḍēn
perumaikaḷ nān vēṇḍēn amararkaḷ nilai vēṇḍēn
aṇimādi siddhikaḷ aṭiyōṭu nān vēṇḍēn
akamatil unaiyenṭrum maravāta nilai vēṇḍum

I don't seek millions in wealth, nor do I seek fame. I have no interest in gaining mystical powers. All I want is to remember You always.

uttama guṇamillai uyarnalan ētumillai
uttamiye untan makanākum takutiyille
sattiyam nī ena nān uṇarntēn tāyē
śankariyē abhayam unaiyanṭri yārumillai

My character is far from noble, and I stake no claim for superiority. I don't even have the right to call myself the child of one as great as You. But I do know one truth: O Shankari, You are my only refuge!

jagadambā jagadambā
jay jagadambā jagadambā

O! Mother of the Universe.

MĀNAS CHŌRĀ RĀDHA KṚṢṆĀ (HINDI)

mānas chōrā rādha kṛṣṇā muralīmōhana saurē
hē yadunāyaka jai giridharī
jasumatinandan pyārē
nandakumarā mathurānāthā
bhajan karē ham tērē

Stealer of mind, beautiful flute player, son of Yashoda, hail to the one who lifts mountains, son of Nanda, Lord of Mathura, Radha's Krishna- I sing Your glory!

tērē pāun paḍē ham kānhā
tū hai hṛdayavihāri hō śyām tū ājā

I bow to Your feet, You reside in my heart.

rādhā kē priya mīrā kē priya
sab kā priyatam hē tū
gōpī vallabha kamsaniśūdana
karuṇāsāgara hē tū
śyāmaḷ tērē rūp nihārē ājā kṛśṇa murārē
kēśava mādhava bansī vādaka naṭavara mērē pyārē
hō śyām tū ājā

Dearest of Radha, of Mira, of the Gopis and of everyone, destroyer of Kamsa, You are the Ocean of Compassion. Dark is Your complexion, O Keshava, player of the flute, dancer, my beloved.

bāngkē bihārī bhayabhavhārī bhaktō kē hitakārī
prēm piyāsē nayan tihārē darśan kō lalchāyē
sundar mangaḷ śyam kaḷebar nandan yadukula rājā
bansī lāl bajākē jaldī ājā mōhan ājā
hō śyām tū ājā

You roam the forests and remove our worldly fears. Protector of the devotees, beautiful, auspicious, dark hued king of Yadavas; play Your flute and hurry here!

MANAVU NONDIRALU AMMA

(KANNADA)

manavu nondiralu amma ni bande tampagi
jagadi bendiralu maguvu ninallave amma
guriyilla daledIralu nī nāde sangāti
berēnu bēdenu amma joteyallave - ninna

When the mind is sad, O Amma, You came cooling it. Are You not the Mother for this child suffering in the world? When I was wandering aimlessly You became my companion. I ask for nothing else, O Amma, other than Your companionship.

iralu hādiyalli ni belaka chellide
bāligāsarē ninnā snehavalla ve
berala hiḍidiralu nī bhayavillanage
bidade rakṣisuvudu amma kṛpayallave - ninna

On the dark path, You shed light. It is not Your love my support for life? When You are holding my finger, I have no fear. It is not Your Grace that protects me, O Amma?

lokamāte āgiralu nī mareteyā – nanna?
kareyali rūvudu ninna madilallavē
jari bīlalu ninna prema setuvā yitu
kaḍala dāti suvudu amma karuneyallave – ninna

O Mother of the world, have You forgotten me? Is it not Your lap which is my refuge? When I was about to fall, Your love became a bridge. Is it not Your compassion that will help me cross the ocean?

MĀNKĀḶI MALLAMMA (KANNADA)

mānkāḷi, mallamma, mādevi mūkāmbā
nūṛāru hesarū devīge
nūṛāru rūpadinannamma tāyī
iruvāḷū nenadora manadāge

'Mankali, Mallamma, Madevi, Mukamba', these are some of the hundreds of names of the Goddess. My Mother takes on hundreds of forms in the minds of those who remember Her.

nannalli, ninnalli, avaḷalli, ivannalli
ellāra oḷagū tānunṭu
ellāra manadā mandiradi kuntāḷe
dharegiḷida avatārī amṛtāmbā

She is in me, in you, in her, in him, She dwells inside every one. The eternal Mother, the incarnation who has descended to earth, resides in everyone's mental shrine.

bīsuva gāḷiya hariyuva jaladhīya
viśāla gaganava noḍalli
ellāva beḷagoḷe ātmada prabhetānu
paramjyoti śivaśakti jagadamba

Look at the blowing wind, flowing water and vast sky; the Mother of the Universe, Supreme Light, who is both Shiva and Shakti, illumines them all through Her effulgent Self.

Śāntiya nīḍuve ānanda nīḍuve
bā nana kandā entaḷe
bāyendu karedū tabbī muddāḍi
ellāra poredāḷe amṛtāmbā

'Come, my child, I will give you peace and happiness.' The eternal Mother hugs us with affection and protects us all.

MĀRĪ KĀḶI MĀ (GUJARATI)

mārī kāḷi mā mārī vāli mā
tanē nihāḷu nihāḷu nihāḷu mā – chāttā
man mārū na bharāyū

O Mother, my dearest Mother Kali, I gaze upon You, Mother, but my mind is never satisfied.

tanē dēkhīnē mā bhaya pāmē ajñānī
tēśū jāṇē mā tū bhayahārini
bhaya hārinī abhaya dāyinī
tanē nihāḷu nihāḷu nihāḷu mā – chāttā
man mārū na bharāyū

Seeing You, the ignorant are terrified, not realizing that You are the destroyer of fears. You free us from all our fears. I keep gazing upon You, O Mother, but my mind is never satisfied.

tanē sōhē galē muṇḍamāla mā
tūttō daittyōnnē haṇanārī
bhavatārinī jagat dhārinī
tanē nihāḷu nihāḷu nihāḷu mā - chāttā
man mārū na bharāyū

A garland of skulls adorns Your neck. You are the destroyer of demons. O Mother, You take us across the ocean of life and death, You are the support of the universe. I keep gazing upon You, O Mother, but my mind is never satisfied.

tāru śaraṇu manē ati pyāru mā
tārā caraṇamā namana karū
bhuvanēśvarī kṛpāsāgarī
tanē nihāḷu nihāḷu nihāḷu mā - chāttā
man mārū na bharayū

O Mother, Your shelter is so dear to me. I bow down at Your holy feet, O bestower of Amrita, ocean of compassion. I keep gazing upon You, O Mother, but my mind is never satisfied.

MĀT BHAVĀNI MAHĒŚI AMBE (HINDI)

māt bhavāni mahēśi ambe
tum hō sabkī mayyā
bhava bhaya bhanjini jana mana ranjini
tum ho jagki mayyā

O Mother Bhavani, great Goddess, You are the Mother of all. You are the one who removes all doubts and fears, and gives joy to all beings. You are the Mother of the whole world!

jay jay jay jagadambē mātē
jay jay jay lalitāmbē mātē

jay jay jay tripurāmbe mātē
jay jay jay kamalāmbē mātē

Victory to the Mother of the universe, victory to the Mother with a pleasing countenance, victory to the Mother of the three cities, victory to the Mother who is seated in a lotus (Lakshmi)!

tum jaga janani tum jaga pālini
jag lay kārani tum hō
tum bhayahārini tum bhavatāriṇi
līlāmayi tum mayyā

The whole universe is born from You; You nourish and sustain the universe; You remove all fears, and help Your children cross the ocean of transmigration. O Mother, Your playfull pastimes are many!

sarjanakāriṇi pālanakāriṇi
śaktisvarūpini tum ho
māyā mōhiṇi mōhanivariṇi
hṛdayavihāriṇi mayyā

You created all the sages and saints, and are the caretaker of every being; Embodiment of power and strength, You destroy our minds' illusion and attachments. O Mother, You reside in the hearts of all beings!

MĀTĀ RĀṆI NE KṚPĀ BASĀYI

(PUNJABI)

mātā rāṇi ne kṛpā basāyi
mērī har gal puri hundi āyi
mātā rāni ne kītti sunvāyi
mērī har gal pūri hūndi āyi

The Empress of the universe has showered Her grace, all my wishes have come true. The divine Mother heard my prayers, all my wishes have come true.

ōne mere sāre rah khōle
mērē sare rukke kāmpūre hōle
mērī mayyā mērī (2)
mērī mayyā mērī sudh len āyi
mērī har gal pūri hūndi āyi

She has cleared all my paths, desires that were blocked have been fulfilled. My Mother, my Mother has come to take my sorrows away. All my wishes have come true.

mātā rāṇi āpe daudi daudi āyi
ōne har kushi mērī jholi pāyi
mērī ambē ne - (2)
mērī ambe ne kītti sunvāyi
mērī har gal pūri hūndi āyi

The Empress of the universe Herself has come running. She has poured all happiness into my pouch. My Mother, my Mother heard my prayers. All my wishes have come true.

ajj mērī mayyā mērē kar āyi
kushiyatte sāgar vich dubki lagāyi
mērī datti ne - (2)
mērī datti ne kītti sunvāyi
mērī har gal pūri hūndi āyi

Today my Mother has come to my house I have taken a dip into the ocean of happiness. My Giver, my Giver heard my prayers. All my wishes have come true.

MĀTHE RAHĒ TĀRO HĀTH MĀ
(GUJARATI)

māthe rahē tāro hāth mā
ā mastak rahē tārā charaṇōm mā
bhūlu na tanē kōyī vātmā
tārū smaraṇ rahē din rāt mā

O Mother, let Thy hand rest on my head, (in blessing). Let my head remain at Thy feet. I should never forget You, for any reason. Your remembrance should remain with me, day and night.

ṭhōkkar hun khāu dvārē dvārē mā
manē śaraṇ tārū ēk sāchū mā
tārā anēk chē upkār mā
tāro kem manū ābhār mā

I have gone and knocked from door to door. In truth, You are the only shelter for me; You have done me so many favors, how shall I express my gratitude to You?

manē ās ēk tārī mā
tārā sīva nathī kōyī mārū mā
tārō karuṇā no nathi par mā
rākhjē sadā tava charṇōn mā

O Mother, You are the only hope for me, there is no one else for me other than You, Your compassion is beyond all limits. Kindly keep me at Thy feet always.

MATIVARUVŌḶAM (MALAYALAM)

**mativaruvōḷam kotitīruvōḷamen
kaṇṇande tirumukham ennu kāṇum? maṇi-
varṇṇande tiruvuṭal ennu kāṇum?**

When will I be able to gaze upon Krishna's divine face to my heart's content? When will I see His holy form?

**kaṇṇande kaṇṇilen kaṇṇum koruttuko-
ṇḍimayanaṅgātirikkyān entu ceyyum? kaṇṇīr
kaṇ nirayātirikkyān entu ceyyum?**

How will I get to look at Him, locking my eyes to His without blinking? How will I keep my eyes from welling up with tears?

**paṭṭupōluḷḷorā pādaṅgaḷ raṇḍumen
mārōṭaṇakkyān entu ceyyum? divya
pādattil cumbikkān entu ceyyum?**

How will I get to hold those feet, soft as silk, close to my breast? How can I get a chance to kiss those holy feet?

**manamaṭaṅguvōḷam matimayaṅguvōḷam ā
mandahāsam kāṇān entu ceyyum? ende
mazhamukilvarṇṇane ennu kāṇum?**

How can I drink in that smile 'till my heart is content, and my mind dissolves in it? When will I see that dear one whose complexion is like a rain-cloud?

**veṇṇayūṭṭām kaṇṇā pālutarām kaṇṇā
kaḷittōzhiyāyennum kūṭe nilkkām, ninde
dāsiyāy ennēyum cērkkū kaṇṇā**

I will feed You butter, O Kanna, I will give You milk! I will stay with You as your playmate! Take me as Your servant forever, Kanna!

MAYYĀJI MENU TŪ CĀHIDI (PUNJABI)

mayyāji menu tū cāhidi
ō dāti menu tū cāhidi
ō dāti menu tū cāhidi
mēri sirte hath rakh dē mā
tu hī mere bhāg jagā ēgi
mayyāji menu ahhā
mayyāji menu ohho
mayyāji menú tū cāhidi
mayyāji menu tū cāhidi
tū har ik pal cāhidi
ō dāti menu tū cāhidi

O Mother, I need You. O giver of all, I need You. Place Your hand on my head; You will awaken my fortunes. I need You, I need You every moment.

tēre nāl hove mērī śām
tēre nāl savēr
mē kadē kalli nā hovā

karde mayyā mēr
akhāde vich hanjū mērē
tūhi menú ākē hasā ēgi
mayyāji menu ahhā
mayyāji menu ohho
mayyāji menú tū cāhidi

mayyāji menu tū cāhidi
tu hi nāl nāl cāhidi
ō dāti menú tū cāhidi

I want to spend my mornings and evenings with You. I never want to be alone; shower me with Your grace. My eyes are filled with tears; only You can make me smile. I need You, I need You with me.

jad vī tērī yād satāve
dil bhar āve mērā
ājā mayyā bhagatt bulāve
chaḍ ke apnā ḍērā
man dī icchā kardē pūri
kado mēnu kōl biṭhā engi
mayyāji menu ahhā
mayyāji menu ohho
mayyāji menu tū cāhidi
mayyāji menu tū cāhidi
mayyāji menú hune cāhidi
ō dāti menú tū cāhidi

Whenever I miss You, come fill my heart with Your love. Your devotee calls You today, come to me and fulfill my desire. When will You let me be with You? I need You, Mother, I need You now.

MĒRĒ HṚDAYA (GUJARATI)

mērē hṛdaya śrī rāma basē
mērā man siyā rāma japē
mērā man siyā rāma jape

Lord Rama resides in my heart. My mind recites the name of Ram.

tum jō hō prabhu dayā kē sāgara
kira kyō khālī mērī dhār ghara
kab lōgē mērī khabara tum ō rām
kē ā na jāyē jīvan kī śām
chal tē chal tē pag hārē
mērā man siyā rāma jape
mērā man siyā rāma jape

You are the ocean of compassion, O Lord, and yet You allow my mind to wander from You. When the sun sets on my life it is You who will then take into account all that I have done. With faltering steps I continue chanting the name of Ram.

rām jī kē bhajana mē hē bal jō baḍā
dvār śabarī kē chalakē ānā paṇā
gū jē hē kaṇ kaṇ lēkē rām nām
rāmā rāmā rāmā rām hē ghana śām nām
chal tē chal tē pag hārē
mērā mana siyā rāma japē
mērā mana siyā rāma jape

So much strength resides in the name of the Lord. Great devotees such as Shabari have received the vision of the Lord Himself. With faltering steps I continue chanting the name of Ram.

MĒRĀ PRĀṆAM HĒ (HINDI)

mērā prāṇam hē mērā prāṇam hē mērā prāṇam he
mā tuhjkō prāṇam he (x2)
mā mujh par kṛpā tu kar dē
mā mujhkō pār karā dē

Salutations Mother, grace me, and take me across.

sārē jahā mē hamārā - ēk
tērā prēm sahārā
kōyī ōr nahī ujiyārā
tērē prēm mē miṭē andhiyārā

In this entire world, my only refuge is Your love. This darkness can be destroyed only by light of Your love.

rāh dikhātā he vō - tērē
pās pahūnchātā he
sukh dilātā he vō - sārē
dukh miṭātā hai

Your love shows us the way, brings us to You, brings happiness and removes all sorrows.

mā jai jai mā, jai jai mā jai jai mā (x5)

Victory to Mother.

MĒRI JHŌPPIDI DĒ (PUNJABI)

mēri jhōppidi dē bhāg ajj khul jānugē
rām ānugē

My small hut will be blessed today. I am fortunate that Rama will come today!

ūṅkā uñch nīch jāt naiyyō vēkhunī
naiyyō vēkhunī
chaṅki chūri visagāt naiyyō vēkhunī naiyyō vēkunī

He will not discriminate between the downtrodden and the fortunate. He will not see caste or social class.

rām vanā vich āyēnē sunukē hā sunukē
nīmē khēṭṭa mīṭhē bēr lāyi chunukē hā chunukē
mēri śardāvalu vēkhu rām bhōg lānugē rām ānugē

Hearing that Rama has come to the forest, I have gathered sweet berries for Him. Upon seeing my devotion and faith, Rama will taste my berries.

mīnnu chajjunī naiyyō nit nēmudā nit nēmudā
mērā vērā vich ras mērē prēmudā
mērē prēmudā
enā khādyāhi rām mērē rajj jānugē rām ānugē

I have no desire for name and fame. All of my being, every vein of my body, is filled with love for Him. By eating my berries, my Rama will be pleased!

MĪṬHĪ MADHURĪ (GUJARATI)

mīṭhī madhurī kānhā tārī muralī
madhura madhura śu gāy āj

O Krishna, which sweet tones is Your flute singing today?

yamunā kinārē rāha jhūye chē
kānhā tārī rādhā āj

O Krishna! On the banks of Yamuna, Radha is waiting for You, today.

sūnī vṛndāvan sūnī chē rādhā
sūnī vraj nī kaṇ kaṇ āj

Vrindavan is lonely, Radha is lonely, lonely is every grain of sand of Vrindavan, today.

rādhā rādhā kahē kānhā nī muralī
tē kēm judā thāy āj

Krishna's murali flute calls out "Radha, Radha!" always. How can they be separated, today.

kānhā thī rādhā dūra nathī kadi
rādhe śyām kahēvāy āj

Radha is never far from Krishna, we sing "Radhe Shyam!", today.

madhur madhur koyal bole
thumak thumak mayur nache
gunj uthi āj madhuban

The nightingale is singing in sweet tones. The peacock is dancing with rhythmical steps. The whole of Vrindavan is echoing with these sounds.

MŌHĀLU CHAMPPARĀ GAURĪ RAMAṆĀ (TELUGU)

mōhālu champparā gaurī ramaṇā
manasuna nimpparā nī smaraṇā

O Gauri Rama (Shiva), kill all my desires and fill my mind with Your memories.

lēru ī jagatīlo nā annavāru
unnadi tōdugā nī ve
madilō uṇḍāli ī bhāvamē
hṛdilō niṇḍāli ānandamē

There is no one in this world to call my own, You are the only companion I have. Let my mind be filled with this feeling. Let my heart be filled with bliss.

hē chandrachūdā hē śūlapāṇi
hē mallikārjjunā nīvē śaraṇam

O one who bears the moon, O one who holds the trident, I seek refuge in Mallikarjuna (Shiva).

ī dēhamē nīkai uṇḍālani
śaktitō nī paninē cheyyālani
nīkai jīviñchuchuṇḍālani
śvāsa nī sēvalō viduvālani

Let my body live for You. Let me have strength to do Your work. Let me live for You. Let me have my last breath in Your service.

MURAḶĪ VĀLE (HINDI)

muraḷī vāle pyāre kānhā
mor mukut dhāri
tum ho sabke hridayavihārī
govardhanadhārī

Dearest Krishna! You play the flute and wear the peacock crown. O, Govardhana (One who held the mountain)! Your play lives within the hearts of everyone.

mukunda mādhava jaya govindā
gopījana kāntā
narakāntaka he nanda dulāre
caraṇa kamal vande

Glory to Govinda, Mukunda, Madhava, the sweetheart of all the gopis! Killer of Narakasura, darling of Nanda, we worship Your lotus feet.

rāsavihārī girivaradhārī
vaijayanti mālī
ākar mere dil me barso
tum karuṇā varī

You delight in the rasa dance; You lifted up the mountain. A garland of wild flowers adorns Your neck. Please come and shower Your grace in my heart!

tum ho bhakton ke hṛdayeśvar
mānasa sancārī
devaki nandana jasumati nandana
tum mangala kārī

Lord of the devotees' hearts, You dwell within our minds. O auspicious one, You are the son of Devaki, and also the son of Yashoda.

gaiyon ke priya gvālon ke priya
sabke chita chorā
tum ho jag ke sirajana hārā
me cākar terā

You are dear to the cows, the darling of the cowherds. You have stolen the hearts of everyone! You destroy all our negativities; I am Your devoted servant.

MURAḶĪ GĀNAMUTIRKKUNNU (MALAYALAM)

muraḷīgānamutirkkunnu hari
vṛndāraṇya-nikuñjē

navarasamadhurima rūkum nava nava-
madhumaya rāgamanōjñam

Krishna is playing His flute in the Vrindavan garden, and His divine music can be heard everywhere, bringing joy to all.

jalavum dharaṇiyum-anilanumoppam
sakalacarācaravṛndam
madhuramanōhara vamśīninadam
pakarum madhu nukarunnu

The water, earth, wind and all of creation on earth are in ectacy listening to the Lord's music.

gopavadhū janavṛndam mādhava-
savidham-aṇaññatiramyam
rāsarāsotsava lahariyilāzhān
lāsyachuvaṭukaḷ veypū

All of the gopis and gopas of Vrindavan gather round Krishna and join in the rasa lila dance.

mama hṛdayattilum-amṛtam peyyum
naṭanam ceyyu! mukundā
mama janmatteyum-alivinnuravāl
amṛtātmakamākku nī

O Krishna! Please come and dance in my heart so that I too will become blissful. With Your compassion, please make my life meaningful by granting me immortality.

MURAḶIKAYILORU GĀNAMUṆḌŌ?

(MALAYALAM)

muraḷikayiloru gānamuṇḍō rādha
śrutimīṭṭi īṇam korukkām
yamunayil ozhukkunna kamalapatrattile
cerukavita nī kāṇmatuṇḍō kṛṣṇā!
muraḷikayiloru gānamuṇḍō?

Is there any song in Your flute? Radha will weave a tune for that. Do You see the small poem in the lotus leaf floating on the waters of the Yamuna river? O Krishna! Is there any song in Your flute?

paḍavukaḷiloru nanavukaṇḍāl – ninde
padakamala malaraṭikaḷōrkkum
niramaya mayilpīlī kaṇḍāl – ninde
kanakamaya tirumakuṭamōrkkum

Seeing the imprint left by the ebbing of the Yamuna river, I will think it is the footprints of Your lotus feet. Seeing the colorful peacock, I will think of Your divine golden crown

mama manasi malinatayozhiññāl – atil
tavacaraṇa malaritaḷ viriññāl
atikutukam anubhūti magnatayiloru putiya
koṭumuṭiyiloru koṭiyuyarnnāl

When the impurities of my mind go away, when Your divine lotus feet open their petals inside me, when I can reach and experience the highest peaks of divine ecstasy and hoist a flag there,

yamunayuṭe ōḷattilāndōḷanam ceyyu –
marayālilayennapōle

anavaratam uṇarvilatulānanda lahariyuṭe
jaladhiyil anāyāsamozhukum

I will dance like a banyan leaf caught in the eddies and currents of the River Yamuna, forever effortlessly lost in the incomparable torrent of bliss.

NĀ MAI DHARMI (HINDI)

nā mai dharmi nā mai dāni
nā mai paṇḍit nā mai jñāni
bas cāhu mai tujhē mā bhavāni
mai tērī hu dīvāni
mujhē chōḍ na dēnā bhavāni

Neither am I spiritual nor a philanthropist. Neither am I knowledgable nor am I a scholar. O Mother Bhavani, consort of Lord Shiva, I am longing for Your love and acceptance. O Mother, please do not forsake me!

nā jānū kōyi vēd aur śāstr
nā jānū mai tap dhyān
bas cāhu tērē caraṇō kō mā
karnē aśru sē snān

I do not have any knowledge of vedas or shastras. I do not know how to do meditation or penance. O Mother, my only desire is to love Your lotus feet. May I bathe in tears of longing for You.

nā cāhu kōyi yōg aur mōkṣ
nā cāhu sukh kalyāṇ
bas cāhu tērē mukh maṇḍal mē
karuṇā ki muskān

O Mother, I desire neither divine union nor salvation. I do not desire any comfort or auspiciousness. O Mother, I desire to see the compassionate smile on Your beautiful face.

nā hai mujhmē sur sangīt
aur nāhi jñān vairāg
bas cāhū mai nirmal bhakti
nij prēm aur viśvās

Neither do I have the ability to sing nor to chant. I only desire innocent devotion, love, and attachment to Your lotus feet.

dē mā bhakti mōh sē mukti dē mā prēm tērā
dē mā bhakti śaraṇ hū tērī dē mā prēm tērā
divy prēm tērā adbhut prēm tērā nirmal prēm tērā

O Mother, grant me devotion and salvation from worldly attachments. Please grant met he love of Your lotus feet. O Mother, grant me refuge. Your love is divine and pure. Bless me!

jay jay jay mā jay jay jay mā jay jay mā jay mā

Victory to the divine Mother!

NAMMAVARĀRŪ NAMAGILLĀ

(KANNADA)

nammavarārū namagillā
ammā nīne namagellā
kāyū nammā dayeyindā
ammā nīne namagellā

None we call 'our' is our own. Only You, O Amma, are our own. Protect us with kindness, You are the Mother of us all.

kattale tumbida manavammā
belakanu chellī belagammā
kainīdi nammanu nadesammā
nīnillade baradammā baradammā

The mind is filled with darkness. Throw light and make it bright, O Mother. Take us by the hand and lead us forward. Without You only barrenness.

nondevu nāvu nāvū bālallī
premava arasī aledihevu
bhaktiya nīḍī harasammā
nīnillade gatiyārū? gatiyārū?

We are sorrow stricken in our lives. We have wandered seeking love. Grant us devotion and bless us, O Amma. If not You, who else is our refuge?

NAMŌSTUTĒ DĒVĪ (MARATHI)

namōstutē dēvī durgē mahēśvarī kāḷī

Devi, Durga, Maheshvari, Kali, our salutations to You!

ambā bhavānī bhagavatī mātā
mantra japunī tuja nāmācā
akhaṇḍa gāū tujhīca gāthā
karū tujhī prārthanā
dēvī karū tujhī prārthanā

Mother, Bhavānī, Bhagavatī, chanting the mantra of Your name and singing Your glories, we pray to You.

jaya jagadambē ambē mā!

Victory to Mother of the universe!

lakṣmī sarasvatī jaya jagadambā
sarvasvarūpiṇī tujhēca cintan
mātē kadhī tū dēśīl darśan
karū tujhī archanā
dēvī karū tujhī archanā

Victory to the Mother of the universe, Lakshmi, Sarasvati! All-pervading one, we meditate only on You. Mother, when will You give us Your darshan? We worship You, Devi, we worship You!

NAIYYĀ TĒRĒ (HINDI)

naiyyā tērē jīvankī
gumrāh kaisē hō gayi
sukhki or nikli thi
dukh sāgarmē khō gayi

How did the boat of your life lose its way? It started its course towards happiness, but got lost in the ocean of sorrow.

tan dhan par hī dhyān diyā
apnē sat kō bisrā diyā
parāyē kō tū apnā samjhā
apnē kō ṭukrā diyā

You paid attention to wealth and body alone, forgetting your true self. You thought a stranger to be yours, forsaking your own self.

ahankār kē jāl mētū
bandi bankar rah gayā
apnē andar kē hīrē kō
pahcānē binā tū rah gayā

In the trap of the ego, you became a prisoner, unable to recognize the jewel inside you.

na sōc din hē bahut
jānē kabh naiyyā dūb jāyē
kāl jō āyē dvār tērē
kal tak tū nahi ṭāl pāyē

Don't think there are endless days; who knows when the boat may sink? If tomorrow comes to your door, you will not be able to put it off to the next day.

NĀN ENNA SEYYAVĒṆḌUM (TAMIL)

nān enna seyyavēṇḍum tāye
un nalmakanāy āvateppaḍi
unakkuṇḍu uttamarāy makkaḷāyiram
atil nalmakanāy āvateppaṭi

What should I do, Mother, to become Your good son? You have thousands of excellent children; how will I also become good?

amudamenum alaikaṭalām tāye
ānandattin nija uruvum nīye
solliḍivāy en arumai tāye
sontam nīyendri vēreyāruḷar

You are the ocean of nectar, Mother, You are the real form of bliss. Tell me my darling Mother, who else do I have to call my own?

enkenkum uraipavaḷē tāyē
endrendrum enai nīnkā tāyē
anpuḷḷam koṇḍavaḷē tāyē
akhilamellām un maṭiyil tānē

O Mother, who shines everywhere, who never leaves my side. O Mother, overflowing with love, the whole world rests in your lap.

NANAGĒNU BĒḌA (KANNADA)

nanagēnu bēḍa nī nalladē
nanagāru bēḍa nī nalladē
ninnaya pādava alladē ō tāyē
nanagēnu bēḍa nī nalladē

O Mother, I don't need anything other than to seek Your feet.

nanagēnu tiḷidilla nanagēnu gottilla
nannavarāru illavē illa
nannēya tāy tandē nīnē
tannēya bandhū baḷakāvu nīnē

I have nothing, I have no one. You are my mother and father, relative and friend.

mandirada oḷigē mūrttiyilla
manada oḷagē nīnē illa
manada mandira oḷagē bandhū
mūrttiyāgu ō tāyē

O Mother, You are the only one in my mind. The temple is empty without an idol - be that idol in the temple of my mind!

NANDALĀLĀ NANDALĀLĀ (SANSKRIT)

nandalālā nandalālā, nandalālā hari nandalālā
navajaladharasamanīla - kṛṣṇa
navajaladharasamanīla

O Krishna, son of Nanda! Your complexion is like a fresh-water rain-cloud.

gōpāla gōpāla
gōpāla gōpāla
gōpijana naṭana vilōla - kṛṣṇa
gōpijana naṭana vilōla

O Gopala, protector of the cows! O Krishna, who loves to dance with the gopis!

ānanda cinmayā gōpāla
gōpāla gōpāla
ātmānanda vilāsā - kṛṣṇa
ātmānanda vilāsā

O Gopala! You are ever blissful, full of only pure thoughts. O Krishna, You are always immersed in the bliss of the Self!

NANNU CŪSI (TELUGU)

nannu cūsi mā tallī
mandahāsamē cēsēnu
madilō mallelu virisēnu
manasu nimgi kegisēnu

Seeing me, my Mother smiled sweetly, and fragrant flowers blossomed in my heart, submerging and uplifting my mind.

tana oḍilōki cērchukunenu
nīvu nā dānivanenu
nī tōḍuga nēnunnānani
cevilō gusagusalāḍēnu

Drawing me into Her lap, She told me I belonged to Her, and whispered in my ear that She would always be with me.

pālavennela kurisēnu
tēli tēli hṛdi murisēnu
nēlapai nākālu niluvakunnadi
gaganamuke nā manasu egiripōtunnadi

Milky moonlight rays poured down, and I floated and frolicked in joy. My feet cannot stay on the ground; my mind is reaching towards the sky.

śivapadamune maripince
tana sannidhine nākichenu
kaivalyadāyakamaina
pādāla cōṭṭunichēnu

Placing me by Her feet that grant liberation, She blessed me with Her presence, so enchanting that the Supreme was forgotten.

ānandagītamē pāḍēnu
paramānandamē pontēnu
nēlapai nākālu niluvakunnadi
gaganamuke nā manasu egiripōtunnadi

Singing a joyful song, I attained supreme bliss; my feet cannot stay on the ground; my mind is reaching towards the sky.

NENE MANAVĒ AMMANA NĪNU (KANNADA)

nene manavē ammana nīnu
ammā ammā enabāradē?

O mind, do remember Amma. Can't you go on calling "Amma. Amma."?

guriyilladē ī bāḷalī alede
elleya mīrī nī manavē!
nillada manavē allilli nīnū
ētake ōdutihe? manavē ētake
ōdutihe?

O mind, you wandered without aim and beyond limits. Unsteady mind, why do you run about here and there? Why?

matiyō jāride manavē nī sōtihe
nemmadi kāṇade oddāḍiruve
iruḷina bēgeya nīguva ammana
kāṇalu bā manavē
manavē kāṇalu bā manavē

My wits have slipped away. O mind, you are vanquished! You are struggling without finding any solace. Come to see Amma who removes the heat of darkness, O mind, come.

NĪ INTRI VERĀRUMILLAI (TAMIL)

nī intri verārumillai – pāvam
inta ezhaikku ammā
innilayil ivane kai viṭuvatu
sarittāno ammā sarittāno?

Amma this poor soul has no refuge other than You. Is it right to abandon me in such a state, O Mother, is it right?

unnai kāttu nān tapamirunten
ennaye mātruvatu saritāno?
nalliravum pakalumunnai venṭi ninṭren – un
tiruppādam maraippatu sarittāno?

Is it right to trick me when I have performed penance waiting for You? Is it right to cover Your divine feet when I have prayed day and night?

un pāsakkaramennai allakkāttiruntu – un
anbu muttam ennai tazhuvayyenkirunten
sellappillai kankkalanka pāttiṭave – tāy
manamurukātiruppatu sarittāno?

I longed for Your loving hug and Your sweet kiss. Is it right to be unmoving and let Your favorite son cry, O Amma?

NINAIVAI NĀN MARAKKAYILĒ

(TAMIL)

ninaivai nān marakkayilē
neñjinilē yār varuvār
nichayamāy nī varuvāy - mattra
mattra ninaivellām akanṭruviṭum

When I forget the inner truth, who will occupy my heart? Surely You will come, and all other thoughts will fade away.

kanavil nān mitakkayilē
kanavukkuḷ yār varuvār
kaṭṭāyam nī varuvāy
mattra kāṭchiyellām maraintuviṭum

As I drift in dreams, who will fill my thoughts? Certainly You will appear in my dreams, all other images will disappear.

uṇavai nān marakkayilē
ūṭṭam tara yār varuvār
uṇavāka nī varuvāy en
uyir kākkum tāyāvāy

Who will come to nurture me when I forget about food? You will come as nourishment, and as the life preserving Mother.

aṇaittiṭa nān ēngugayil
ādaravāy yār varuvār
ammāvām nī varuvāy
aṇaittu entan tuyar tīrppāy

As I yearn to be hugged, who will come as my support? O Mother, You will come to hug me and end my sorrows.

uyirāy uṇarvāy vazhiyāy oḷiyāy
guruvāy gatiyāy varuvāyē
anpāy amutāy aṇaippāy
arivāy aruḷāy varuvāyē

Please come as my life, perception, path, light, guru and destiny. You are love, nectar, knowledge. Please hug me and shower Your grace!

NINNA MAMATE (KANNADA)

ninna mamate prītiyalli
nānu karuṇe kaṇḍēnu
ihada nōva maretēnu
parada kaḍegē olidēnu

In Your compassionate love, I forget the pain of this world and seek the path to the Supreme.

ninna pālige nānu kanda
adē nanage ānanda
ninna maḍilali oragide
ninna sparśake sukhiside

Being Your baby is my joy; resting in Your lap, I long for Your touch!

dhanyavāyitu nanna baduku
ammā ninna neneyuta
nīniralu neravige
janma pāvana ennuta

My life is blessed by memories of You; my birth has become sanctified by Your supportive presence.

NINTRA TIRU KOLAM KANTEN

(TAMIL)

nintra tiru kolam kanten
nirai tiruppādam kanṭen
anṭralarnda malarai pola
akam kulirum siripai kanṭen

I am focused on Your beautiful form and Your divine feet, I see Your smile as charming as a freshly bloomed flower, and that calms my mind.

alail aṭikku kanṭen
karaittanil aṭanka kanṭen
alai pāyum entan manamum
annai anbil aṭanka kanṭen

I see the waves lashing but contained by the shore, just as Your love contains my wandering mind.

ilaikal asainda potum
iruvizhikal azhaikka kanṭen
mazhaittulikal vīzhuntapotum
manakkarunai vellam kanṭen

Even when the leaves move, I am reminded of Your inviting eyes. Even as the rain drops fall, I see the flow of Your compassion.

unna nān unaveḍuttāl
un mukhame atilum kanṭen
enna nān ninaitta potum
en ammā unnai kanṭen

Even as I begin to eat I see only Your face in the food; whatever may be my thoughts O Mother, I only see You in them too.

NĪ TANDA SOLLEṬUTTU (TAMIL)

nī tanda solleṭuttu nān pāṭinēn
nilaiyaṭṭra vāzhvirkku poruḷ tēṭinēn
nān enṭrum nī enṭrum ēn pārppadō
nān unnil karaindiṭa nāḷ pārppadō

I sang with the words You gave me; I searched for the meaning of this illusory life. I think that You and I are separate; should I be thinking of the day when I will merge in You?

yandiramāy nānum iyankīṭinum
iyakkiṭum śaktiyinṭri iyakkamuṇḍō
seyalgaḷai nānum seydīṭinum
seyalpaṭum valimai unadanṭrō

Though I move around like a machine, I should know that even a machine needs power to operate. Though I perform many actions, I should realize that the power to act comes only from You.

viralkūṭa nīyinṭri asainditumō
vīṇāy ārpparittal maṭamaiyanṭrō
ulakattin asaivellām unadanṭrō
umaiyaval un pādam śaraṇamanṭrō

We criticize our karmas because of our foolishness. Even a finger will not move without You. All of the activity in this world is Yours alone. O Mother Uma, I seek refuge at Your feet!

ŌM HARI ŌM HARI (TAMIL)

ōm hari ōm hari ōm hari ōm hari
ōm hari ōm hari ōm hari ōm

ōm hari ōm hari ōm hari ōm hari
ōm hari ōm hari ōm hari ōm

Om Hari, Om Hari.

jñāniyar yōgiyar ṛṣikaḷ solli tanta
mantiram praṇavam ōm
ōmenum tārakam uṛaittiruntāl
vēṛoru chintanai illai enbōm

The primordial sound OM is the mantra from the wise, yogis and rishis. If one chants OM no other thoughts can arise.

tārakamantiram vēdattin sāram
puṇyabhūmi tantadāl

pittanai pōlatai nittamum japittu
chittam teḷindu inburuvōm

It is the essence of the Vedas gifted by the pure land. Constant chanting like a deranged man purifies the mind.

uḷḷattin kōvilil sadā pūyaikaḷ
dīpārādhanai nadakkumē
sadā pūjaikaḷ nadappatālē
nanmaikaḷ viḷaiyum kōdiyē

Constant prayers in the temple of the mind can only bring goodness in plenty.

kōti kōti kōṭi eṇṇaṅkaḷ oṭuṅki
orumukamāy ākumē
orumukamāy āvatālē
pērinbam vantu sērumē

Many many thoughts disappear and transform to one pointedness bringing forth permanent happiness

OM MANGALAM (SANSKRIT)

om mangalam
omkara mangalam
om namah śivaya
śri gurave mangalam

Om is auspicious, the syllable Om is auspicious. Salutations to Shiva. Sri Guru is auspicious.

na-mangalam
nakara mangalam
nada bindu kalātita
gurave mangalam

Na is auspicious, the syllable Na is auspicious. The guru who is beyond sound and all form is auspicious.

ma mangalam
makara mangalam
maya moha bandha rahita
gurave mangalam

Ma is auspicious. The syllable Ma is auspicious. The guru who is beyond maya and all attachment is auspicious.

śi mangalam
śikāra mangalam
śiva viṣṇu brahma rūpa
gurave mangalam

Shi is auspicious. The syllable Shi is auspicious. The guru, who is in the form of the Trinity – Shiva, Vishnu, Brahma – is auspicious.

vā – mangaḷam
vakāra mangaḷam
vāda veda jñāna dīpa
guravē mangaḷam

Va is auspicious. The syllable Va is auspicious. The guru who is the light of knowledge, of all debate and learning, is auspicious.

yā – mangalam
yakāra mangalam
yāga yoga sākṣibhāva
guravē mangalam

Ya is auspicious. The syllable Ya is auspicious. The guru, who is witness to all action and sadhana is auspicious.

amba mangalam
jagadamba mangalam
annapoorne śankarāngi
śakti mangalam

Mother, the Mother of the world is auspicious. She is the granter of food, She is the better-half of Shiva, She is Shakti.

amba mangalam
jagadamba mangalam
mahalakshmi śaradambe
kali mangalam

Mother is auspicious. The Mother of the world is auspicious. She is Mahalakshmi, goddess of prosperity. She is Sharadamba, goddess of learning. She is Kali, goddess of dissolution.

amba mangalam
jagadamba mangalam
brahma rupe viśva rupe
devi mangalam

Mother is auspicious. The Mother of the world is auspicious. She is the form of ultimate Brahman, She is the form of the universe. She is Devi, She is auspicious.

OM ŚAKTI (TAMIL)

om śakti om śakti om – parāśakti
om śakti om śakti om
om śakti om śakti om – parāśakti
ādi parāśakti om

Obeisance to the supreme power of the universe. Obeisance to the primordial energy of the universe.

ammā nān unnai marandālum
tāyē nī ennai marappāyō
kattrariyā uḷḷam tanai kaḷvanaippōl māttrinēn
pattrukaḷāl pāsamgaḷāl pāṭham kattruttērinēn
tīmaiyaitterindiuntum tīvinayāl keṭṭēn
nanmai ena arindum arukē pōnatillai

O Mother, even if we forget You, will You forget us? I've secretly tainted my pure and pristine heart. As a result of attachments and bonds, I have learned many lessons. Even though I knew it was bad, I did what was wrong. Even though I knew what was good, I did not act, and thus sullied my character.

nān ariyātennuḷḷē pukundu naṭattukirāy
nān arindēn ena ninaittāl pāṭāyppaṭuttukirāy
meypporuḷām dēvi unnai arivatu eḷitō
poyyulakam tannil ennai pōkaviṭātē

Without my knowing it, You steal into my heart and operate from within. If I think I know You, You crush my ego. Is it easy to fathom You, O Devi, the embodiment of truth? Please do not let me get lost in the world of falsehood.

OM ŚAKTI OM ŚAKTI OM ŚAKTI

(TAMIL)

om śakti om śakti om śakti om śakti
om śakti om śakti om śakti om (x2)
ālayamani isaikka manikkatavum tāzhtirakku
mangalavādyattin oli keṭkave
vedaghoṣam etirolikka devagānam enkum
keṭka

śrī simhavāhini praveśīttāle

As the temple bells ring, as the sanctum sanctorum door opens, as the divine music is heard, as the Vedic chants reverberate and as the celestial beings sing, Devi, who commandeers a lion, makes Her entrance.

anbukoṇḍu kankalanki artthamulla vāzhv venṭa
aḍimai ennai kannasaittu aravanaippāle
veru enna venḍum jīvan janmasāphalyamākum
svayamprakāśam āna kāli entan annaiye

As this slave longs for a meaningful life with tearful eyes, She hugs me with approving eyes. What else is there in life other than liberation from the cycle of birth and death, O Kali, my Mother, the self illuminating one?

icchaiyellām pūrttiśeytu kālam virayam ākkum mune
venṭamai venṭi tāyai śaran pukuvome
śvāsam muzhutum kalantiṭuvāl idhayam śuddhamākkiṭuvāl
āsaiyenḍra sollukkini iḍam illaye

Instead of merely fulfilling all our desires and idle away our life, let us pray to the Mother for the state of no desires. She will then become our very breath and purify our heart thus denying any place for the wants.

ŌMKĀRA SVARARŪPIṆĪ UṆARŪ (MALAYALAM)

ōmkāra svararūpiṇī uṇarū
nī eṇḍe hṛdayāntarāḷangaḷil
mṛdutantriyil oru mantramāyi
ātmāvil varaviṇayail unarū
ōmkāra svararūpiṇī

Awake, O form of the cosmic sound, as a sweet mantra in my heart, resonating to the chords of celestial vina in my soul.

āhlādaniraviṇṭe malarvādiyil
sāmōdamādum mayūripōle
ānandanarttanam āḍān ninakkeṇḍe
jīvitārāmamorungi nīḷe

Like the gracefully dancing peacock in the grove of ecstasy, dance the dance of bliss in the prepared venue of my life.

pāṛiparakkuna pūttumbipōl - kāttil
pāṭi kaḷikkunna pūvallipōl
kākaḷipāṭunna pūñchōlapōl - pāṭi
yāṭittimarkkukenn ātmāvil nī

Like the flitting butterfly among gracefully swaying creepers and swishing bunches of flowers, you dance and sing in my soul.

ŌMKĀREŚVARA (TELUGU)

ōmkāreśvara kailāseśvara
hara hara mahāprabhō
naṭanā manōhara śrī paramēśvara

śiva śiva mahāprabhō

Oh lord of the divine syllable Om, lord of Mount Kailash, Hara, great God! Enchanting dancer, supreme lord Shiva!

śriśaila vāsā śrī pārvatīśā
hara hara mahāprabhō
śrī nīlakaṇṭhā śrī bhūtipūrṇṇā
śiva śiva mahāprabhō

Lord of Parvati, divine One who resides on Mount Kailash! Oh Shiva whose throat is blue, full of divine glories, Shiva, great Lord!

viśvēśvarā dēva mṛtyuñjayāhara
hara hara mahāprabhō
mōkṣa pradāyaka mōhāndhya nāśaka
śiva śiva mahāprabhō

Lord of the universe, conqueror of death, who bestows liberation and destroys the darkness of delusion, Shiva, great Lord!

mahāpāpa nāśana sadā suprasanna
hara hara mahāprabhō
bhavat pādapat mam sadāham namāmi
śiva śiva mahāprabhō

Destroyer of sins, ever gracious Lord, I bow down always at Your lotus feet! O great Lord, Siva!

hara hara mahāprabhō śiva śiva mahāprabhō
ōmkāreśvarā śiva śiva śankara
kailāseśvarā śiva śiva śankara
naṭanamanōhara śiva śiva śankara
śrī paramēśvara śiva śiva śankara

gangādharahara śiva śiva śankara
mṛtyuñjayahara śiva śiva śankara

O Lord of Omkara, bestower of auspiciousness, Lord of Kailash, great dancer, supreme Lord, bearer of the Ganga, conqueror of death, O great Lord Shiva!

PAGALAINA RĒYAINA (TELUGU)

pagalaina rēyaina karigēṭṭi kṣaṇamaina
nītalapē yada niṇḍani – ō jananī
nī nāma śudha poṅgani

Day and night and in every fleeting second, let thoughts of You pervade my heart. O Mother, may my heart overflow with the bliss of Your divine name.

nālōna lōlona molakettu bhāvlu
pūbālalai viriyanī – ō jananī
nī padamulē tākanī

Let the budding emotions in the deep recesses of my heart bloom like a garden of flowers; O divine Mother of the universe, may Your feet tread on them!

māṭṭalō, cētalō pāṭalō pilupulō
nī caraṇamē śaraṇanī – ō jananī
neranammī madi koluvanī

With faith and devotion in my heart, O Mother, let me surrender at Your feet in my speech, action, and song.

tanuvēmō kōvelai manasēmō dīpamai
bhaktibāṭṭanu sāganī – ō jananī
amṛtadhārala grōlanī

With my body as Your temple and my mind as a sacred lamp, let me follow the path of devotion. O divine Mother of the universe, let me drink the nectar of Your bliss.

ilalōna kalalōna janmajanmala lōna
nanuganna tallivanī - ō jananī
mudamāra ninu cūḍanī - ō jananī
muripāna oḍi cēranī

In this world, in dreams, and in lives to come, as my eternal Mother, O divine Mother of the universe, let me always find You in my heart and joyfully reach Your divine lap.

PĀHI PĀHI DĒVI PĀHI (TELUGU)

pāhi pāhi dēvi pāhi antunēni
dēhi dēhi dēvī ī pāda dāsiki bhakti
ī pāda dāsiki bhakti

I am just the servant of Your holy feet. Help me to attain true love for You.

nāri teliyaka allāḍēnu
velugē chūppi kāpāḍavē
entaintu tirigēnu
nī padamulanē chēruṭṭaku

I wander aimlessly, not knowing the way forward. Shine Your light on my path and protect me. How far have I wandered in the search of Your holy feet?

agni mēghālu chuṭṭēnammā
māya yēva variñchēnammā
annī telisina talivi ammā
dukhamē bāppi rakṣiñchavammā

I am engulfed in clouds of fire. Illusion surrounds me. All knowing Mother, dispel my sorrow and grant me Your protection.

PAṆDURĪTSĀ DĒVĀ TUJHI (MARATHI)

paṇdurītsā dēvā tujhi ārati ōvāḷūdē
śyāmā tujī kṛpā sadā āmhāvarī rāhūdē
āmahāvarī rāhūdē

O Lord Panduranga, I wave the sacred lamp before You. O Lord with a dark complexion, may Your grace be always upon me.

hāth tujī kaṭṭēvarī anagāvari pītambar
jīvamāssā charaṇī tujā kṣan bharī māzzādēvā
anandāt rāhūdē ānandāt rāhūdē
śyamā tujī kṛpā sadā āmahāvarī rāhūdē
āmahāvarī rāhūde

You have bangles on Your hands and Your body is attired with a yellow garment. Every moment of my life is dedicated to Your lotus feet. O Lord, let me always dwell in this bliss. O dark One, may Your grace and mercy ever be upon me.

rakh māyīssā devā vaso rūp tujā lōcanī
śōkpīddā charṇī tujē kṛpā sadā māzzā dēvā
āmhāvarī vāhūdē āmhāvarī vāhūdē
śyamā tujī kṛpā sadā āmahāvarī rāhūdē
āmahāvarī rāhūde

O Lord of Rukmini, how graceful is Your form. Bless me that I may always remain at Your feet. O dark One, may Your grace and mercy ever be upon me.

sukh thōd duḥkh bhārī duniyā hī bhalī burī
kaṣṭāssudhā tujē manan satat mī māzzā dēvā
ānandānī karūdē ānandānī karūdē
śyamā tujī kṛpā sadā āmahāvarī rāhūdē
āmahāvarī rāhūde

There is more sorrow than pleasure in this world full of pain and suffering. However much torment I may go through, O Lord, in my mind and heart may I always remember You. Lord, please let me do this, please let me do this with joy. O dark One, may Your grace ever be upon me.

PARABRAHMA (KANNADA)

parabrahma prabheyāda paramjyōti
nannamma
śyāmalavarṇṇini dhavaḷāva guṇṭhini
nīyārendu nā hēḷali
ninna mahime ēnendu nā hēḷali
ninna mahime ēnendu nā hēḷali

My Mother, You are the shining light of supreme Brahman. How can I express who You are, how can I describe Your glory?

mōhaka kaṇṇōṭṭa beṇṇe kaḷḷana āṭṭa
kānalu bālle nijadali māte
līlāvinōdini ammā
guṇagaḷigatīte ammā

With enchanting glances, the butter thief's (Krishna's) games, innocent looks of a girl, You are a true Mother; You are beyond the three gunas.

śiradali mukuṭa jaratāri sīre
īgomme kāḷi magadomme lalite
ellāra snehite ammā
śivaśakti ekyavē ammā

With crown on Your head, wearing a grand sari, sometimes You are Kali and sometimes You are Lalita. You are everyone's friend, Mother, You are the oneness of Shiva and Shakti.

sāgarakū gūḍa gāḷigū saraḷa
śiradali bēṭṭa karmadi gangē
nirantara vāhini ammā
sṛṣṭiya dāsānudāsi ammā

More mysterious than the ocean, subtler than the air, like a mountain in steadfastness, and like Ganga in action, Amma, You are eternally flowing and serving the whole of creation.

līlānāṭaka sūtra khēlanakari
mandasmita vadane prēmāvatāri
amṛtānandamayi ammā
sadguru rūpiṇi ammā

My smiling Mother of immortal bliss, my Sadguru, love incarnate; You are the controller of this play of creation, O Mother!

PAṬṬAVE PĀDAMU (TELUGU)

paṭṭave pādamu gaṭṭigā manasā
paṭṭunu viḍuvaka niluvave manasā

O mind, hold onto Her feet with all your strength, stay there and don't let go.

penumāyala tera kamminagāni
palumārlu guri tappinagāni
suḍigālulu celarēgina gāni
bhavasāgaramuna munigina gāni

Although the dark heavy veils of maya surround you, although we may so often miss the goal, although tornadoes rage around you, even if you drown in the ocean of this world - hold on to Her feet.

śaraṇāgatulanu kāceḍi pādamu
bhaktajanulanu brēceṭi pādamu
nammina biḍḍala sākeḍi pādamu
viśva rūpamuna veligeḍi pādamu

Those feet protect whoever surrenders to You; they grace those who are devoted to You and nourish the children who believe in You. Those feet illumine the creation, showing it to be a manifestation of the cosmic form.

sṛṣṭiki mūlamu ā mṛdupādamu
hariharabrahmalu koliceṭi pādamu
muggurammalaku mūlapu pādamu
amṛtapadamu gamyamu pādamu

Those sweet feet are the primal cause of creation. They are worshipped by the trinity, and are the base of the three mothers. Those feet are the goal of the path to immortality.

PĒLAVA KAIVIRAL (MALAYALAM)

pēlava kaiviral tumbilppiṭichu ñān
sānandam unmattanāyi
ninnōṭorumichulāttān kotikunnu
nīle chidākāśa dēśe

I long to walk together with You along the vast, open space of consciousness. Happy and excited, I will take hold of Your soft fingertips.

kālanīr chālonnu nīntikaṭannu ñān
prēma sāmrājya tilettān
pūpōl mṛddutvam manassinne zhāmamma
pilinētra tāluzhiyū

By swimming across the ocean of time I may at last reach the kingdom of love. May my mind become as soft as a flower when caressed by Her eyes that resemble peacock feathers.

ēkāntamākumī jīvitāraṇyaka –
pātayil kāliṭarāte
nērttoru nulveṭṭamenkilum nīṭṭumō
nīyente nīrmizhikumbil

Please shine a ray of light in my eyes so that I am guided steadily along this lonely path of life that is like a forest.

nīrum neruppum virudhadharmmam pole
dēhidēhaṇgalum bhinnam
dēhō habhāvam poliññu bhāram kura
ñānamikkaṭṭe nin kālkal

Just like water and fire so are the body and the Self different from one another. Let me lose the weight of the notion "I am the body" and salute Your feet.

āmnāya jñāna chaitanyamē – ennile
ñānayo rānanda sindhō
dhyānōr jarēṇu pravāhattilūṭe ñān
tēṭunnu nin prēmatīram

Vedic knowledge, consciousness, is the truth within me; it is the ocean of bliss. Through the light that flows in my meditation I explore Your ocean of love.

PRĒMA SĀGARA (KANNADA)

prēma sāgara ninna mānasa sarōvarā
manassina cintēya nīgisuva sangītā
hṛdaya spandisuva mauna sandēśā
samarppisuvē nanna ī jīvitavu ninnalli

The lake of Your mind is like an ocean of love, like a gentle music soothing the turbulences of the mind. Your silent messages touch the heart; I offer my life to You.

ēkāntanāgi andhakāradalli cintisalu
ninna divya amṛtasāgara sēridē
amṛtatva sēvisalu hṛdaya spandisitu
ninna divya caraṇavē duḥkha nivāraṇavu

I was wandering lonely in deep ignorance- I came across Your divine, immortal ocean. My heart was touched, hearing Your immortal teachings. Your holy feet are the only cure for all misery.

ō ānanda sāgarā ninna svarūpā
dēhābimānā biḍisu dēvi mā
jñānajyōti beḷagu nanna cidrūpiṇī
mahāyōgini amṛtēśvarī ninna mahāsāgarā

O! Your real nature is divine bliss! Release me from the body-mind complex, O Goddess- light the lamp of knowledge, You whose form is consciousness absolute. You are the supreme yogini, eternal Goddess, in the ocean of love.

PRĒM HI JĪVAN KĀ ĀDHĀR HĒ (HINDI)

prēm hi jīvan kā ādhār hē
prēm har ēk dharm kā sār hē
prēm sē miṭ tā ahankār hē
prēm sē har bēḍā pār hē

Love is the pillar of life. Love is the essence of dharma. Love destroys the ego. Love helps us to cross the ocean of illusion.

prēm mē kyā jīt hē kyā hār hē
sukh kyā dukh kyā har pal tyōhār hē
prēm sē hi satya sākṣāt kār hē
prēm sē miṭ tā anḍakār hē (2)

In love, there is no victory or defeat. Love makes both sorrows and happiness feel like celebration. Love takes all our miseries away, and love wipes the ego away.

manvā prēm kar, kar sab sē tū pyār
svarg ban jāyē sansār

O Man, love, love everyone! When we spread love, the world will become like heaven.

mānē jō jag kō prēm sē parivār hē
kartā har bandē ko jō svīkār hē
upkār kartā jō sabkā satkār hē
aur kaun vō? īśkā avtār hē (2)

Whoever loves the world as one family, and accepts everyone as his own, whoever works for the well-being of others, and whoever respects all beings, is the incarnation of God.

PUKĀRĒ MAYYĀ TUMHĒ SADĀ HAM

(HINDI)

pukārē mayyā tumhē sadā ham
tumhī kṛpā kar hamē bachāvo
karō kṛpā mā karō dayā mā (2)

Mother, we are always calling You. Show mercy and save us! Show mercy, Mother, show mercy!

tumharē darśan binā bēchārē
hamārē dil yē taras rahē hē
virah kī āg mē taḍap rahē hē
ō mā jay jay mā
daras tū dēkar pyās bujhā dē

Our wretched hearts pine for Your darshan, burning in the agony of separation. Give us your darshan and quench this thirst. O Mother, victory to Mother

bicchaḍ kē tum sē taṭap taṭap kar
pukārē mayyā tumem sadā ham
chātak jaisē kab sē pyāsē
ō mā jay jay mā
ab to maiyya darś dikhao

Separated from You I pine and continuously call for You, Mother. We are thirsty like the chataka bird; at least now give us Your darshan, O Mother.

SĀKĀ VARAMARUḶVĀY RĀMĀ (TAMIL)

sākā varamaruḷvāy rāmā
caturmarainātha sarōjapādā

O Rama! You with lotus feet, Lord of the four Vedas, bless me with immortality!

ākāsantīkāl nīrmaṇ
attanai bhūtamum ottu niraintāy
ēkāmṛtamākiya nintāḷ
iṇaisaraṇeṭrāl itu muṭiyātā

You are the embodiment of the five elements. If we surrender at Your feet, which are the very embodiment of bliss, may we not receive Your blessings?

vākārtōḷ vīrā dhīrā
manmadarūpā vānavar būpā
pākārmozhi sītaiyin menṭroḷ
pazhakiya mārbā padamalar sārbā

O courageous Rama, with a sublimely beautiful form, with beautiful shoulders as strong as bamboo! O King of the celestials, whose consort Sita's speech is sweet as honey! Your lotus feet are sought for surrender by all.

nitya nirmalā rāmā
niṣkaḷankā sarvādhārā
sadayā sanātanā rāmā
saraṇam saraṇam saraṇamudārā

O Rama, You are immortal, pure, unblemished, omnipotent, the eternal embodiment of Truth! I bow down to You, merciful Rama!

jay jay rām sītārām

Victory to Rama, Sita's beloved!

ŚAKTI TĀ JAGADAMBĀ (TAMIL)

śakti tā jagadambā
bhakti tā jagadambā
anbai tā jagadambā
nambikkai tantennai kāttiṭuvāy

O Mother of the Universe! Give me strength, give me devotion. O Mother of the Universe! Give me love. Give me faith, and protect me!

anaittuyirum nīyena nān
anmbuṭan paṇi puriya
aṇuvēnum nīyinṭri
asaiyātena uṇarum
bhakti tā jagadambā

O Mother of the universe! Grant me devotion that will enable me to serve all living beings with love, and see them as Your form. Nothing, even an atom can move without You.

nikazhvatellām nin seyalāy
nittam ninaindurugum
anbai tā jagadambā

O Mother of the Universe! Give me supreme love, that my mind may melt every moment with the knowledge that everything in this world is Your leela (divine play).

tāy karattil piḷḷaiyena
dayavuṭan kāppāy ennum
nambikkai tantennai kāttiṭuvāy

O Mother! Give me the faith that You will protect me with compassion, just as a mother cradles her baby in her arms.

SANKAR SUT HŌ TUM (HINDI)

sankar sut hō tum - sare
sankaṭ har lō tum
dās tumhārō dēv – ham kō
vāncchit var dō tum

Child of Shankara (Shiva) remove all my problems. I am Your servant, bless me.

vāraṇ mukh dēvā gaurī
nandan gajvadanā
vighnēṣvar varadā sundar!
gangādhara tanayā

O Elephant-faced child of Gauri (Parvati's son), remover of obstacles, beauteous one, son of the bearer of Ganga.

musē par chaḍhakar - āvō -
māyā mōh harō - sārō -
mangal ham kō dō – tumhī
ēk sahārā hō

Come, seated on a mouse, remove illusion and infatuation. Bestow auspiciousness. You are my sole refuge.

siddhivināyak tum – jaldī
siddha karō sab kām
balihārī tērē – har lō
vighna hamārē tum

O Siddhivinayaka, make my actions fruitful and remove all obstacles.

ŚANKARĀ ŚIVA ŚANKARĀ (TAMIL)

śankarā śiva śankarā śankarā śiva śankarā
ponnum poruḷum tēḍi ōḍi
ponnāna kālatte pokka vēṇḍām
innum iruppatu ettanai nāḷ
nī arivāy pon ambalavāṇā

O Shiva Shankara! O Man, do not waste your time seeking gold and wealth. Only the Lord who resides in the Golden Palace knows how many more days are left in your life.

vēṇḍāta vambellām vāṅgikoṇḍu
vemmāya kāṭṭile vīzhāmal
ōḍiye vantu un seyiney taḍuttu
kālam kaṭattāmal āṭṭu koḷḷuvāy
śankarā śiva śankarā śiva śankarā śiva śankarā

O Shankara! Please come to me fast and protect me so that I do not spend my days wandering in this forest of delusion, subjected to all kinds of gossip.

tēḍiya neñcirkku tēnāy inippāy
vāḍiya payirkku uyar nīrāvāy
āḍiya pādattāl āṇavam akattri
nāḍiya ēntan uḷḷam niravāy
śankarā śiva śankarā śiva śankarā śiva śankarā

O Lord Shankara! To Your seekers, You are as sweet as honey! You rejuvenate faded crops. Please come dancing to me, fill my mind (with joy) and destroy my ego.

ŚARAṆĀGAT KŌ APNĀVŌ MĀ (HINDI)

śaraṇāgat kō apnāvō mā
mujkō śaraṇ me lēlō mā
rāh batā dō mā iskō
śaraṇ mē mā me ā sakū
tērī mahimā mē gā sakū

Take me in Your refuge, Mother. Show me the way! Allow me to take refuge in You, Mother; allow me to know Your glory!

mā ō mā pukārū mē tērā hī guṇ gāvū mē
tērē sumiran sē nit mā
sacchā dhan bas pāū mē

Mother, I call out Your name, I sing Your glories, and by remembering You always, I will acquire real wealth!

sōtā sōchū mā kō mē
jāgā sōchū mā kō mē
sukhō mē sōchū mā kō mē
duhkhō mē sōchū mā kō mē
mā kō hī sōchū mē

I think of You while sleeping and while awake. I think of You in happiness and in sorrow. I think only of You, Mother!

mē yādō kē phūl chadāū
aur āsu kē dīp jalāū
man mandir mē tujhē biṭhāū
tum kō pāū tum mē samāū
tum kō hī pāū mē

I offer You the flowers of memories, I light the lamp of tears. I install You in the temple of my mind; may I attain You, merge in You. May I attain only You, may I merge only in You, Mother!

sōttā sōchū (jay jagadambā)
jāgā sōchū (jay jagadambā)
sukhō mē sōchū (jay jagadambā)
duhkhō mē sōchū (jay jagadambā)
jay jagadambā jay jagadambā

I remember You while asleep, victory to the Mother of the Universe! I remember You while awake, victory to the divine Mother! I remember You in happiness, I remember You in sorrow. Victory to the Mother of the universe.

ŚARAṆAṆṬI ŚARAṆAṆṬI (TELUGU)

śaraṇaṇṭi śaraṇaṇṭi dēvi nī śaraṇaṇṭi
akhilalōkamulēlu amma nī śaraṇaṇṭṭi

O Devi, I take refuge in You. O Mother, ruler of all the worlds, I take refuge in You.

kaluva kannulalō karuṇa kurippiñcinā
kōpamuttō kanulu erajesi cūsinā
nanu broche callani tallivani nammiti
amttaṭa dēvi nī caraṇamule śaraṇaṇṭi

Whether You pour out compassion through Your lotus eyes, or You look at me angrily, I believe that You are the Mother who will always protect me and therefore I take refuge at Your feet, O Devi.

kaṇṭiki reppalā kāpāḍedavani
kanureppalārppaka kāvaluṇṭāvani
kannulu terippiñcedavanī nammati
amttaṭa dēvi nī caraṇamule śaraṇaṇti

I believe that You will protect me like eyelids protecting the eyes, guard me without even blinking Your eyes, and open my eyes to the Truth and therefore I take refuge at Your feet, O Devi.

SARVAVYĀPIYĒ (TAMIL)

sarvavyāpiyē sarvavyāpiyē sadā
eṇṇumpōtē sukam manatil perukukintratē

O omnipresent one, O all-pervading one, Your constant remembrance brings peace of mind.

sambavankal ezhuti vaittāy parampōruḷē nī
mātri ezhuta nān muyaṇtrāl naṭappatā atu
avaravarkku vidhittu vaittatavāravārkku nān
atai anubhavikkumpōtu nammai aṛivatu
nantra - anda

You decreed the experiences, O primordial one! Is it possible for me to change Your will? Experiencing Your will is a path to realize the Self.

kaṇṇīrkondu prārthanaikaḷ karaikondu
sērkkum
matimayakkam iṭaiyil vantu vazhimaṛikkum
kiṭṭātāyin veṭṭena maṛappatu nanḍru – bhāvam
taṭṭāmal bhagavaniṭam sērkkumē enḍru – anda

Tearful prayers will take us ashore; delusions on the way will present obstacles. It is good to forget immediately that which we will not get in the world. That attitude will certainly take us to the God's abode.

sākṣibāvam āḷumpōtu nittirai kalaiyum
sattiyam jayikkumpōtu viṭiyalill muṭiyum
mukti entra ariya ninlai yārukku puriyum - nal
bhakti maṭṭum pōtum pōtum jñānam piṛakkum
- anda

Living in the self removes all dreams. Victory to the truth will end in dawn. Who understands the state of liberation? Devotion alone is enough to attain enlightenment.

ŚARAṆŪ ŚARAṆŪ (KANNADA)

śaraṇū śaraṇū embē gaṇanāthā
gajamukha dēvanē gaṇanāthā

I surrender to You, Lord of the Ganas, the elephant-faced God!

ādyādi pūjita āmōda dāyaka
vidyēya nāyaka buddhi pradāyaka
vighna vināśaka vandanē
gaṇanāthā gaṇanāthā
gaṇanāthā gaṇanāthā

Salutations to the one who is worshipped first, the giver of happiness, the Lord of knowledge, the one who grants wisdom and removes obstacles.

gītēya rāga nī gānada bhāva nī
nāṭya viśārada sundara swāmi nī
ōmkāra rūpa nī gāndhāri

You are the tune in the song, You are the essence of music, You are the expert dancer and the beautiful Lord, You are the form of Om.

mūṣika vāhana mōdaka priya nī
mahadēva tanayā pārvati putra nī
mamgaḷakara nī gurudēva

You ride on the mouse, You are the lover of modaka sweets, son of Shiva and Parvati. You are the teacher and the source of auspiciousness.

SILUKISADIRU NĪ (KANNADA)

silukisadiru nī ī lōkadi - enna
silukisadiru nī ī lōkadi

Do not let me be caught in this world.

bandhana bēḍige bedari nā baḷalide
bhaktiya muktiya nīḍenage

I am frightened of the handcuffs of attachment. Hence grant me devotion and liberation.

sūryanu beḷakina maneyante - nīnu
arivina beḷakina gurumāte
manadali manemāḍi marevege dūḍi
nagutide nōḍamma māyāndhakāra
nagutide nōḍamma māyājālā

Just as the sun is home to all light, You are to the light of Knowledge, O Mother Guru. The darkness of Maya, this net of Maya, has secretly made my mind its home, caught me up in forgetfulness, and laughs at me, teases me. See, Mother!

rāgadi biḍisu vairāgyadi nilisu

mōhadi biḍisu premadi nilisu
kāmane biḍisu karuṇāmṛta harisu
śōkadi biḍisu śaraṇāgati nīḍu

Release me from attachment. May I be established in detachment.Release me from attachment. May I be established in love. Release me from desire. Let the nectar of immortal bliss flow from You. Release me from sorrow and grant me surrender.

SOLLARIYA NIN PUKHAZHAI (TAMIL)

sollariya nin pukhazhai solvateppaḍi
sollariyā siru mazhalai enna seyvatu
sollukellām poruḷ tarum enta sol ētu
sollum taṛum inimai tarum ammā enbatu

I am a small child with no words. Wordless, how can I sing Your praises? The word which gives meaning to all words is the sweet word, "Amma"; it gives sweetness every time we utter it.

ul manatil olikkum kural ētu
aṭikkaṭi nām azhaikkum oli ētu
akhilam ellām iyakkum āttral ētu
nammai arukiruntu kākkum ammā allavā

The voice that rings in the inner mind, the name that we often call; the power behind this world is "Amma", who protects us, staying close by our side.

vān mazhai eṅkum pozhivatu pōl
varum kātru eṅkum vīsiṭal pōl
bhūmittāyi anaittaiyum poṛuttiṭal pōl
nānilattil nalla tuṇai ammā nīyentrō

Just as the sky showers rain everywhere, just as the wind embraces everything, just as Mother Earth patiently bears everything, Amma, You are our true companion in this world.

ŚRI GAṆANĀYAKA (HINDI)

śri gaṇanāyaka! hum hai
terī śaran main āye
tū karūṇākar hum pe
vighna sabhi harlenā

Lord Ganesha! I seek refuge in You. Please shower Your grace on me and remove all my obstacles.

jay jay gaṇapati devā
suramuni vandita caraṇā
jay gajamukha varadātā
jay girijāsuta sukhadā

O great Ganesha, whose feet are worshipped by celestials and sages, who has the face of an elephant! Son of Parvati, daughter of the mountain, You grant every boon and every pleasure.

siddhivināyaka hai tū
nirmal mati ke dātā
vidyā vijay sabhī hai
terā dān gaṇeśā

You are the master of all siddhis (special powers); You grant us clean minds and the boons of knowledge and victory.

tu rakṣak bhaktōn ke
vighna vināśak pyāre
hum caraṇon main tere

karte naman hasārōn

O dearest one, protector of the devotees, remover of obstacles! We prostrate a thousand times at Your feet.

ŚRI LAḶITĒ (TULU)

śri laḷitē ēnklēna
dēvare īrappē
prēma bhakti korlappē
jīvana dēvarū īrappē

Sri Lalita, You are our Goddess, You are our Mother. Grant us love and devotion. You are our Goddess, You are our very life.

karuṇāmayī īrappē
kāppīyarana bhattinappē
kārttigē dinaṭṭu bhattinappē
kāpōṭatte īrappē

O Mother, You are the embodiment of compassion. On the day of Karthika You came down to protect us, O Mother, You must save us!

laḷitē laḷitē śrī laḷitē
ēnkḷena dēvare īrappē

Lalita, Sri Lalita, You are our Goddess, You are our Mother!

ŚRĪVEṄKAṬĒŚA (TELUGU)

śrīveṅkaṭēśa śrīvāsōlakṣmīpati praṇāmam
amṛtāmśō jagadvandyō gōvinda śāśvataprabhō
śēṣādrinilayō dēvā kēśavō madhusūdanaḥ
amṛtō mādhavaḥ kṛṣṇā śrīhariḥ jñānapañjaraḥ

Salutation to Lord Venkatesha, the Lord of Goddess Lakshmi. The Lord whose nature is nectar, who is worshipped by the universe, who protects all beings, and who is all-pervading. The One who sleeps on the serpent Shesha, destroyer of Madhu, the essence of eternal knowledge!

sadā veṅkaṭēśam smarāmi smarāmi
harē veṇkatēśam prasīda prasīda
priyam veṇkaṭēśam prayaccha prayaccha
śrī veṇkaṭēśam namāmi namāmi

I always remember the holy name of Lord Venkatesha. O Lord Venkatesha, kindly be pleased. Dear Lord, please bless me! I worship Lord Venkatesha.

yōgīśahṛdaya śāśvatanivāsō
sakalāmanōbhīṣṭa suphalapradātā
śritajanapōṣā abhayapradātā
mām pāhi mām pāhi punitapadakamalam

He always dwells in the hearts of yogis, and fulfills all the desires of His devotees; He is the sustainer of those who take refuge in Him, and makes His devotee fearless. I take refuge at the lotus feet of Lord Hari.

dēvādhidēva jagadēkasvāmi
śrī śrīnivāsa sarvvāntaryāmi
hē bhaktavatsalā dīnadayālō
mam pāhi mām pāhi punitapadakamalam

O Lord of the gods, Master of the Universe, in whom Lakshmi resides, who dwells in everything. He loves His devotees and uplifts the downtrodden. I take refuge at the lotus feet of Lord Hari.

vēdāntavēdyam nigamāntasāram
kāruṇyapūrṇṇam kamaladaḷanayanam
nētrānandam mamgaḷasvarūpam
mām pāhi mām pāhi punitapadakamalam

The Lord who is to be known through the Vedas, essence of eternal knowledge, ever compassionate, whose eyes ressemble lotus petals, and whose form is auspicious - I take refuge at the lotus feet of Lord Hari.

ghōrasamsāra sāgarasētu
vīrasudhīra mōkṣaikahētu
pūrṇṇaprabhōllāsa nijavaibhavāmgā
mām pāhi mām pāhi punitapadakamalam

The Lord who is the bridge to cross the ocean of birth and death, who purifies the devotees' hearts and helps them attain salvation, the fully resplendant One. I take refuge at the lotus feet of Lord Hari.

sadā veṅkaṭēśam harē veṅkaṭēśam
priyam veṅkaṭēśam namō veṅkaṭēśam

Always Lord Venkatesha, victory to Lord Venkatesha, beloved Lord Venkatesha, salutations to Lord Venkatesha!

SUNDAR HAI NĀYANĀ TERE (HINDI)

sundar hai nāyanā tere, kānhā
madhur madhur bol madhur madhur bol
murali kī dun mē tērī, nāchē
man kā mōr yē man kā mōr

O Krishna, how beautiful are Your eyes! Your speech and voice are full of sweetness. Upon hearing the sound of Your flute, the peacock of my mind started to dance in bliss.

jādu yē kesā kiyā jāduyē kesā kīyā
sabko mōh liyā
mākhan chor mē dil ko churā liyā

Krishna, what magic have You done? You have enchanted the mind of everyone. O butter thief, You have stolen the hearts of everyone!

dēkhā jab pehli bār dēkhtē hī rah gayē
khushiyo kē sāgar mē, behatē chalē

When I first saw You, I could not take my gaze away. I was immersed in an ocean of bliss.

man mē basē ho śyām, honton pē tērā nām
dikhe aur kuch nahi, tērē sivā ghanaśyām

O Shyam, You dwell in my heart, only Your name is on my lips. I cannot perceive anything other than You, O dark complexioned One.

har gōpi har gval bolē
lahar lahar jamunā kī bolē
dharttī kā har kan bi bolē
vraj sāra ik svar mē bolē
hari bol hari bol hari bol hari bol
hari bol hari bol hari bol hari bol

Every milkmaid and every cowherd boy, every wave of the Yamuna river, every speck of dust, the whole of Vraj (the homeland of Lord Krishna) is singing in unison "Chant the name of Lord Hari!"

SUNDARI JAGANMŌHINI (KANNADA)

sundari jaganmōhini kuḍi nōṭava bīrutali bā
ātma samsātake bā bāreyā karuṇāmayi

O beautiful one, O enchantress of the world! Do come, throwing love-glances. Give companionship to my Self. Won't You come, O Mother of compassion?

mangaḷē sukhakāriṇi janma pāpavināśini
enna mārgadarśini bhavāniye mṛdubhāṣiṇi
ambike jagadambike janma pāvani dēviyu ni
ninna maḍilali malagisiko kōmalē vimalāmbikē

O auspicious one who comforts, O one who destroys the sins of this lifetime. O one who shows me my path, O Bhavani, O soft spoken one! O Mother, O Mother of the world, You are the Goddess who makes our lives blessed. Take me in Your lap, O sweet one, O Mother who is pure.

candrikē bhavatāriṇi bhava bandhana biḍisutali
nava santasa nīḍuta bā bāreyā jaganmāteye
śāradē vidyādēviye jñāna dēviye vandisuvē
nīḍu bhaktiya varavēnagē dēviyē paramjyōtiyē

O Mother, cool like the moonlight, O Mother who takes devotees across the world of transmigration, release me from all worldly ties. Give me new joys, come. Won't You come, O mother of the world? O Sharada you are the goddess of learning. You are the Devi of knowledge. My prostrations to You. Grant me the gift of devotion, O Devi, the highest, resplendent one.

lakṣmiyē kamalāmbikē ellā sṛṣṭiya oḍatiyu ni
kaiyya mugiyuta vandisuvē māteye
mamatāmayi
durgiyē lalitāmbikē nitya prēma kaṭākṣavē bā
satya jyōti prakāśavē bā kāḷiyē amṛtēśvari

O Lakshmi, the goddess bearing the lotus, You lord over all of creation. I join my hands and bow to You. O Mother who is full of love for Your children! O Durge, O Lalitambike. O the one who throws love-glances all the time, do come. O the light of Truth, O Kali, O Amriteshwari, come.

SVARLŌKA VĀTSALYA DHĀRĀYAI

(MALAYALAM)

svarlōka vātsalya dhārāyai
nīṛunna jīvende dāhangaḷil
tōrāte peyunna kāruṇyamē
nī tanne nanmatan pon pratīkam
nī martya janma sāphalya sāram

O flowing stream of heavenly love! You are an unending rain of compassion in my aching thirsty life. You are the very embodiment of goodness, You are the essence of the goal of human life.

ninnil nin oru nāḷ oramṛtaraśmi
aṛiyāte akatāril vīṇaliññu
uyir tingum aśrubindu kalake
atil minni māṇikyamāy chamaññu
nī tanne nanmatan pon pratīkam
nī martya janma sāphalya sāram

Once, from You a ray of immortal light unknowingly fell and melted into my being and, shining through the teardrops of my life, became precious gems. You are the very embodiment of goodness, You are the essence of the goal of human life.

aparāśrudhārayil manamuruki
avirāma makhilātma śānti tēṭi
uṟaviṭum prēma muḷḷil tuḷumbi
ulakāke niṟayuvānāyi vembi,
nī tanne nanmatan pon pratīkam
nī martya janma sāphalya sāram

My mind melts in an intense flow of tears. All souls search for peace in this twilight. The love inside now overflows and yearns to flood the world. You are the very embodiment of goodness You are the essence of the goal of human life.

naipuṇyamēlāttavar tannilum
nī puṇya karma chāturyamēki
lōkōpakāraika chittarākum
tyāgōtsukar ākkiṭunnu nityam,
nī tanne nanmatan pon pratīkam
nī martya janma sāphalya sāram

Your wondrous good deeds even for the undeserving turn my mind to thoughts of serving the world, making me eternally selfless. You are the very embodiment of goodness, You are the essence of the goal of human life.

ŚYĀM ŚYĀM KŪKADĪ MĒ (PUNJABI)

śyām śyām kūkadī mē
āpē śyām hō ga yī
śyām tērē vās tē mē
bad nām hō ga yī

Calling out to Shyam I have come more and more to resemble Him. For His sake my own reputation has suffered.

īk vārī ājā śyām jān na dēvā mē
jān na dēvā mē
dil ap nē nū tōkhā khān na dēvā mē
khān na dēvā mē
duniyā vī tak kē hē rān hō ga yī

O Shyam, please come before me at least once or I will give up my life. Do not deceive my heart. This world has become amazed seeing my condition.

bāsurī tērī nē śyām kaisā jādū pāyā hē
kaisā jādū pāyā hē
pōlī pālī rādhikā dā man śara māyā hē
man śara māya hē
bāsurī tērī tō mē kur bān hō ga yī

Shyam, what magic resides in Your flute! Even the heart of innocent Radha becomes shy. I have given up everything to hear the sound of that flute, Shyam!

TAPAMANU (TELUGU)

tapamanu dhanuvanu cēpaṭṭu
manasanu śaramunu sandhiñcu
brahmamanu lakṣyamu bhēdincu
ēkatvamune sādhincu

Take up the bow of austerities, fix the arrow of mind, shoot the goal of Brahman, and gain oneness with Brahman.

bhavabandhamulu māyākaṭṭlu
gaṭṭivi vāṭini tempuṭṭaku
puṭṭuṭṭa giṭṭuṭṭa kāraṇamaina
pāpapuṇyamula tolagiñcu

Worldly bonds are illusory bondages, but very strong and difficult to cut free. Rid yourself of both merit and sin; they are responsible for the cycle of birth and death.

manasulō cintalu malinamulu
madilō dēvuni marapiñce
maruguna paṭina mādhavu neruga
avidya teranu tolagiñcu

Thoughts in the mind are like dirt covering up the Lord inside the heart. Remove the curtain of ignorance, to find the veiled Lord.

TATHI TATHI (TAMIL)

tathi tathi naḍandu varum cellammā – manam
taḷir naḍayil makizhndiḍute ponnammā
koṇci koṇci pēsumbōdu cellammā – inbam
miṇciḍumē nēṇcuvaiyai ponnammā

O darling Mother, who walks with toddler steps, my heart feels joy seeing Your gait. Your speech is sweeter than nectar, O darling Mother!

tūvi vaittēn pūvin mettai cellammā – irundum
piñcu pādam sivanta daṭi ponnammā
tānkavillai neñcamaṭi cellamma – inda
pūkkaḷellām mōsamaṭi ponnammā

My darling Mother, I sprinkled soft flowers for You to tread on, yet Your soft feet became red, Oh golden Mother! I am unable to bear this, dear Mother, for even these flowers are not soft enough for You, my golden Mother!

vaikkum aḍi ovvonṭrilum cellammā – nī
vettripera vēṇumaḍi ponnammā
undanadu sēvaiyonṭrē cellammā – enḍrum
enkaḷadu sādhanayē ponnammā

My darling Mother, may You become victorious in each and every step You take! My darling Mother, our only spiritual practice is to do Your divine work!

ēzhulōka mahārāṇi cellammā – nī
enkaḷukku mātārāṇi ponnammā
enḍrenḍrum un nalamē cellammā – vēṇḍum
enkaḷadu idayamaṭi ponnammā

My dear Mother, You are the Empress of the seven worlds, but to us You are our supreme divine Mother! Our hearts always yearn for Your well being, oh darling Mother!

ōḍi vā cellammā nī āḍi vā ponnammā

Come running to me, darling Mother! Come dancing to me, golden Mother!

TEḌAL THOḌANKUM (TAMIL)

teḍal thoḍankum deyva teḍal toḍankum
toṭanki viṭṭāl akattinil vichāram naṭakkum
kankal tirakkum karunai pirakkum
muṭivinile niśchayamāy nargati kiṭaiykkum

The search begins and the search for God begins. The search promotes quest inside. The eye of compassion opens up. Eventually the soul will be uplifted for sure.

sūkṣmamāy ārugunankal patunkiyirukkum
toṭṭuviṭṭāl ezhum kopakkanal parakkum
sadguruvin tunaināḍa arul surakkum
puyalukkuppin peramaiti onṭru pirakkum

The six attributes (lust, anger, greed, intoxication, pride, and jealousy) will remain latent. Instigation brings out the fire of anger. Seeking the Sadguru will result in Grace. An extreme peace will be born after a heavy storm.

unarvukalin āzhattil tirukkural keṭkum
manasākṣiyāka eppotum monattil irukkum
darmmavazhi naḍakkinḍra yāvarkkum keṭkum
nalvinaippayanāle ellām sirakkum

The divine sound will be heard deep within. That is the witness that ever remains in silence. The sound can be heard by all those who follow righteousness. All will flourish as the fruits of good deeds.

ādiparāśakti potri
vaṭiveṭuttu vanta tāye potri
uruvirku appāl uraipaval potri
ellāmum āna annaye potri
potri potri potri potri

Glory to Adi Parashakti. Glory to the One who has taken the form of Mother. Glory to the one who is beyond all forms. Glory to the one who is everything. Glory, Glory, Glory!

TĒRĀ AKṢARĪ MANTRA (MARATHI)

tērā akṣarī mantra japāvā
dhyānī manī śrīrāma rāma
śrīrāma jayarāma jayajaya rāma
śrīrāma jayarāma jayajaya rāma

Chant the mantra with thirteen syllables for Sri Rama, while working and in meditation.

daiva tujhē hē tujhyā na hātī
sōnyācīhī hōtē mātī
uratī pāp mag daiva hātī
thēvā smaratō rāma rāma

With the power of the mantra you will control your luck; without the power of the mantra, when you are left to deal with your sins, then you will remember Lord Rama.

śraddhā ṭhēvā dēvāvaratī
mātīcē kaṇ suvarṇa banatī
lōkāsāṭhī jagāt jagatī
jīvanī tyāncyā rāma rāma

Have faith in God, and even dust will turn to gold. Live your life to serve others, and your life will be guided by Lord Rama.

kausalyāsut ayōdhyā rāma
bhajanī rangē śrīrāma rāma
jīvanī aisā rangalā rāma
śrīrāma jaya rāma jayajaya rāma

Son of Kausalya, King of Ayodhya, Rama! Contemplate on His form and sing 'Sri Rama, Rama'! Fill your whole life with Rama!

TUJHYĀTA VIṬHALA (MARATHI)

tujhyāta viṭhala māzhāta viṭhala
sarvā bhūti viṭhala rē
jagāt kari tū prēmcha kēvala
kunnī vēgala nāhī rē

Vithala is in you and in me. Vithala is in every being. He has only love for all in this world. Nobody is separate from Him.

viśvātīla kaṇā kaṇātūni
harīcha bharalā āhē rē
kālātīla kṣaṇā kṣaṇā tū nī
haricha kēvala āhē rē

Each and every particle in this universe is filled with the Lord Hari. In every second of time there is only Hari.

samśaya sōḍūnī sagalē ātā
harinām tumhi ghyāvē rē
tāril tumhā sarvāmmadhuni
ananya ṭhēvā bhāv rē

Leave all doubts aside and chant the name of Hari. Take refuge in Him alone; He will save you from all harm.

tujhyāta viṭhala viṭhala viṭhala
māzhāta viṭhala viṭhala viṭhala

Vithala is in you and in me.

TUNPANKAḶE (TAMIL)

tunpankaḷe vāzhvil ellai entrālum
unpadam piṭikkinḍra varamontru tā
kaṣṭankaḷ unniṭam serkkumentrāl tāye
kaṣṭatilum nī dhairyam tā

Even if I must have troubles until the end of my life, please grant me the boon that I may forever hold on to Your feet. If it is only through suffering that I can merge in You, then please give me the courage to face it.

kaṇkaḷum kulamāgum
atiloru sukham vaittāy
ovvoru muttilum tirumukham kāṭṭi
anpuṭan enai pārttāy
padam maṭṭum teḷiyavillai – ēnō
kal manam kaniyavillai

My eyes overflow with tears; even in that experience You give sweetness. With every tear drop, Your loving gaze is upon me. I don't know why I can't see Your feet clearly, why Your heart of stone refuses to melt.

kanavinile untan
arukinil kaḷikkintren
tiruvaṭi padinta mannil puraṇḍu

azhutiṭa ēnkukiren
āvi pirintiṭumō - enne
arave marantat ēn

In my dreams I come close and enjoy being near You. I long to cry and roll on the sand that has been blessed by the touch of Your lotus feet. Will my soul leave this body before experiencing that? Why have You completely forgotten me?

TUMBIKKAIYĀN TUṆAIYIRUPPĀN
(TAMIL)

tumbikkaiyān tuṇaiyiruppān
tuyartanai pōkki vaḷam taruvān
nambikkaiyōḍu tutippōrkkē
nāḷum avanē nalam taruvān

Vinayaka, the elephant-faced Lord, always protects me. He is the remover of sorrows, and grants all goodness. He bestows blessings on those who pray with faith.

vēda poruḷāy viḷaṅkiṭuvān
vettrikaḷ anaittum kuvittiṭuvān
nāda rūpa vināyakanē
nammai enṭrum kāttiṭuvān

He is the source of the Vedas and the cause of all victories. O Vinayaka, Embodiment of the primordial sound, protect us forever!

ārumukhanin sōdaranē
akhilam kākkum pūraṇanē
kūrum aṭiyār vinai tīrppān
kuñjara mukhattān gaṇanāthan

O brother of the six headed Lord Muruga, protector of the universe! He erases the devotees' past misdeeds, and is the leader of all the gods.

piravi peruṅkaṭal nīṅkiṭavē
pemmān mandiram ōdiṭavē
araṅkaḷ sirandu vaḷarndiṭavē
ambikai bālan aruḷ taruvān

As righteousness is spread everywhere, and as we cross the ocean of birth and death, imbibing divine teachings, the blessings of the son of Parvati are upon us!

pārvati maindā pāpa vimōchakā kāttiṭuvāy dēvā

Oh Lord, son of Parvati, destroyer of sin, please protect us!

UNDAN NĀMAM (TAMIL)

undan nāmam pāḍi pāḍi pāḍi varuven
undan rūpam kanḍu kanḍu kanḍu makizhven
ammā ammā ammā

I come singing Your glory and I become blissful watching Your form. O Mother, O Mother, O Mother.

unnara ke nāṭiyye ōṭi ōṭiye varuven
unnoṭu onṭrāy āṭave virunbuven
ennuḍan nī pāṭi āḍuvāy
amma

I come running to be near You. And I desire to dance along with You. Please sing and dance along with me, O Mother.

un iniya nāmankal manatil niraintu niraintu
un iniya gānattāl sevikalum kulirndu

ennuḍan ni vilaiyāḍuvāy
ammā

Your sweet names fill my heart and Your melodious songs are pleasing to my ears. Please play with me, O Mother.

unnai ninaindu ninaindu kan nanaindu
nanaindu tuti pāṭuven
unnaṭiyin on uṭay innaindiṭa pirunbuven
ennal enuṭum nī niraindiṭuvāy
ammā

I shed tears as I think about You and sing Your glory. I long to rest on Your lap. Always be with me, O Mother.

en jīva jotiyum bivya oliyum nīyānāy
pon polivu tūvum avvilakkum nānāven
pozhindiṭuvāy un arulai
ammā

You are my life and the divine light within. I am a lamp that sheds that golden light. O Mother, please shower Your grace!

UNMATTA PAÑCAKAM (TAMIL)

unmatta pañcakam pāṭiṭuvēnō
janmattin payan tanai tēṭiṭuvēnō
eṇpattum oru viradam irundiṭuvēnō
kaṇpotti kaḷikkum kaṇṇā nī solvāy

Will I sing five hymns that were written in divine intoxication? Will I attain the purpose of human birth? O You who play hide and seek, tell me.

solvatellām seyvatuṇḍō
seyvatellām solvatuṇḍō
uyyum vazhi ētum uṇḍō
un pādam tozhuvatanṭrō
tozhuvatonṭrē vazhiyākum
azhuvatu tān abhiṣēkam – atu
kazhuvum pāvamellām – atil
karayum vinaikal ellām

Do we do whatever we say? Do we say whatever we do? Is there any way to transform myself? Your lotus feet are the only way for transformation; the only way is to worship You. My tears, a ceremonial worship to You, will remove all my sins. My karma will melt away in that worship.

vinai tīrndāl ānandam
sollāmal akattil varum
akattil uḷḷa ānandam – enṭrum
azhiyā pēttrai tarum
pēratanai nān peravē
perumai migum padam paṇindēn
pērinbam nilai peravē
piḷḷai unai caraṇ pukundēn

When all my sins are absolved, inner peace will come to me of its own accord. That bliss alone will give immortality. To attain immortality, I worship Your honored lotus feet and take refuge in You.

VANAMĀLI KAṆṆĀ (MALAYALAM)

vanamāli kaṇṇā nin māṛilē mālayil
oru tuḷasi daḷamāyenkil ñān

nin kazal patiyunna bhūmiyiloru – cheṛu
maṇtari enkilumāyenkil
maṇtari enkilumāyenkil

Kanna, if only I were the tulasi leaves of the garland that adorns Your chest. If only I were a grain of sand on the ground blessed by the touch of Your feet.

kaṇṇande rūpam smarikkunna mātrayil
kaṇṇunīr ozhukunna mizhiyāyiṭām
nī kavarnnuṇṇunna tair veṇṇayāyiṭām
nin kālkkalarcchikkum pūvāyiṭām

Let me be the eye which will drop tears at the mere thought of Kanna's form. Let become the ghee that You will eat. Let be the flower that will be offered at Your feet.

nin muṭichūṭum mayilpīliyiloru
varṇṇamāyenkilum chērniṭām ñān
kaṇṇā nī ūti uṇarttunna kuzhalil
nallimbamēṛunnoru gānamākām

I will merge at least as one of the colours of the peacock feather that adorns Your hair. Oh Krishna! I will become a melodious tune from the flute that is played and awakened by You.

entākilum kaṇṇā ninnilēkkaṇayuvān
vembal koḷḷunnoru manamēkiṭu
veṛude janicchu marikkāte nin nāma
tīrthattāl pāvana janmamākkū

Whatever it is Kanna, please give a mind that has the longing to merge in You. Instead of simply going through the cycle of birth and death, please purify this life with the holy water of Your name.

VARUGĀ VARUGĀ (TAMIL)

varugā varugā ammā varugā varugā

Come! Come! Mother, come! Come!

enkaḷ unmai selvam nī ammā varuga varuga
kaṇṇukkeṭṭātu dūrattil nī sentrālum
nittam nittam enkaḷ cittattil
undan ninaivukaḷ

You are our real wealth, Amma, come! Come! Even if You go far away and out of sight, every day, in our mind, we only think of You.

ettanai manankaḷ evaḷavu yēkkankaḷ
vimmi azhum idayangaḷ yērāḷam
kāṇa tuṭikkum enkaḷ kaṇgaḷakku
muzhu nilavāy vārum ammā vārum

O Mother, why haven't You come yet? How many minds have been yearning for You, how many hearts weeping for You! Our eyes are trembling to see You. Please reveal Yourself to us, like moonlight.

koñcamum mārādu un punnagai mukham
koñcamum vāṭātu un malligai guṇam
pārkku pārkku paravaśam aḷikkum
anpin vaṭivamē varuga varuga

Your smiling face never changes. Your behaviour, fragrant as jasmine, never fades. O Mother, embodiment of Love, who immerses us in joy, come, come.

VARUMŌ INIYUM (MALAYALAM)

varumō iniyum ituvazhi orunāḷ
iviṭeyī vṛndāvanabhūmiyil - ende
manassinde vṛndāvanavāṭiyill!

Will You come once again, this way, here in this place of Vrindavan- the Vrindavan garden of my mind?

vazhimaṛannālum smaraṇakaḷ ninnuṭe
kazhalaṭikaḷeyingānayikkum – prēma
tapassinde havissu nī svīkarikkum!

Even if the way is forgotten, the thoughts will lead Your legs towards here- You will accept the oblation offered in the tapas of love.

akrūranennōru pērōtivannayāḷ
etrayum nirddayanāyirunnillayō?
akkoṭum krūrataykkinnum pratīkamāy
kandriṭāmātmāvil tēruruḷcchālukaḷ!

The one who came with the name of Akrura (not-cruel)- was He cruel like that? The marks of Your cruelty, can be seen in my soul even today!

annārathachakram āzhnnuvindundāya
randām yamuna nī kandālaṛiyumō?
rādhatan neñchile lāvayāṇā jala
dhāraykkuṛavayennāraṛiyicchiṭum!

Will You realize that the Yamuna river was split in two by the wheel of that chariot (in which you left)? Who is there to tell You that the fountain in the Yamuna is from Radha's overflowing heart?

allenkilentinnitellām kathikkunnu
antarangamkondu randalla mādhavan
pullāmkuzhalile pallavi nīyenkil,
santatam ñānanupallaviyallayō?

Or else, what is the need in saying all this- I am not separate from Madhava inside. If You are the pallavi of the flute, will I not always be its anupallavi?

(pallavi refers to the chorus or leading verse of a song and anupallavi to the portion of the verse next to it.)

VEDANA KOṆḌORU (MALAYALAM)

vedana koṇḍoru muḷamkuzhal tīrttu
kaṇṇīru koṇḍoru yamunayozhukki
ōrmmatankanalukaḷ neṇcōṭu certtitā
kāttirikkūnnī puzhayuṭe tīrattu

From pain I created a bamboo flute, and my flowing tears formed a Yamuna river. I waited on the banks of that river, the burning embers of pain in my heart.

ninakkāy karutiya mayilpīlitaṇḍukaḷ
niramvārnna manasil ozhiññiruppū
ninakkāy karutiya duritattinnavilitā
citalarichen meni vālmīkamāvunnu

The colors of the peacock feathers I had kept for You in my heart are fading away. The puffed rice I had prepared for You has become a festering mound of sorrows that surrounds me, like Valmiki, buried in an anthill while doing penance.

varikilleyennālum kaṇṇā ninnormmayil
kazhiyunnu dvārakayil – ennum
manasinde dvārakayil

Oh Kanna, will You not come? I am always dwelling in thoughts of You, in Dvaraka, the Dvaraka of my mind!

ninakkāy karutiya arayālinnilakaḷum
azhalin venalil kariññuṇaṅīḍunnu
ninakkāy karutiya kunnikkuruvukaḷ
vīṇḍum taḷirttu niṇamazha tūvunnu

The banyan leaves I had kept for You are shriveling, burning in the scorching summer heat of sorrow. The red kunni seeds that were meant for You are again sprouting, causing a drizzle of blood, as it were.

varikillayennālum kaṇṇā ninnormmayil
kōḍijanmam taraṇe ariyān
kōḍijanmam taraṇe ariyān

Even though You might not come, Kanna, please grant me a hundred lives spent immersed in thoughts of You, searching for You. Grant me a thousand births that I may know You.

VEṆṆILĀ VADANAM (TAMIL)

veṇṇilā vadanam veṇṇira āṭaiyil
uditta uraintatai en solvēn

How can I describe my Mother, whose face is like moonlight, who is dressed in white?

akhilam viyakkum anpukoṇḍu
avataritta poruḷ en solvēn
kāṇpavar neñcattai kavarntē izhukkum
kāntavizhiyai en solvēn

How can I describe this being who is the incarnation of love, who fills the universe with wonder? How can I describe those eyes that draw the devotees minds to them like a magnet?

nāṭutōrum nāṭichenṭra nanmai
purinta nayattai en solvēn
bhuvanam ariyā kurumbu punmuruval
pūtta putumai en solvēn

How do I describe that goodness that travels all over the worlds? How do I describe that mischievous smile that the world can never really understand?

mūkkuttiyil minukkum minnal
oḷiyin vanmaiyin vakaiyariyēn
dinamum tiruvizhākāṇum dēvimun
tikaikkacheyta tiramariyēn

I do not understand the greatness of the lustre of Your nosering. I stand in awe in front of Devi who is like a festival every day!

ammā inkē vā vā vā āṇḍaruḷ purintiṭa vā vā vā
ammā inkē vā vā vā āṇḍaruḷ purintiṭa vā vā vā

Mother! Come, come, come here. Bless me! Bless me! Bless me!

VILVATTĀL ARCHITTŌM (TAMIL)

vilvattāl archittōm
viśvēśā kāttiṭuvāy
allal tarum tuyar nīṅka
amṛtēśā kāttiṭuvāy

We perform the Vilvam flower worship, O Lord of the universe, protect us! Remove the pain of suffering, O Amritesha, please protect us!

vāzhvennum piṇi tīrttu
vaiddīśā kāttiṭuvāy
vāzhvāṅku vāzhavaittu
vaiyyakattai kāttiṭuvāy

O Vaidisa, please remove the pain of this human life and protect us. Make this human existence happy and peaceful, always bestow Your protection in this world.

śivanai nān vaṇaṅkukirēn
śivappadattai tandiṭuvāy
araṇ unnai vaṇaṅkukirēn
anbu neñjai kāttiṭuvāy

O Lord Shiva, I bow down to to You, that You may grant me that Eternal state. This devotee is bowing down before You; please show me Your kind heart!

śiva śiva śaṅkara gauri manōhara
charaṇam śaraṇam sarvēśā
śiva śiva śaṅkara gauri manōhara
charaṇam śaraṇam sarvēśā
śiva śiva śaṅkara gauri manōhara
śiva śiva śaṅkara gauri manōhara

O Shiva, Shankara, who is adored by Gauri (Parvathi). Lord of all, I take refuge at Your feet.

VINĀYAKANE VINAY TĪRTARULVĀY
(TAMIL)

vināyakane vinay tīrtarulvāy
vaḷangal peruka vāzhkai shezhikka

Please remove the obstacles so that my life may blossom and good fortune may come to me.

om enum mandira
vaḍivam tāngi vandāy
odum maraikalil
uṭporulāki ninḍrai

Your form itself carries the message of the mantra 'Om'. You are the essense of the four Vedas.

malaimakal maindane malaraḍi nāḍukirōm
aḍiyavar manadinil nimmadi nilaittiḍa

O son of Parashakti, I come to Your lotus feet. Give this slave of Yours peace of mind.

vēzha mukham kanḍāl vēdanai tīrndiḍumē
vēnḍum varangalum vēnḍāmal kiḍaitiḍume

When we look at Your elephant-like form all our sorrows vanish. Even without our asking, You will give all that we need.

ulakattin nāyakane uvappuḍan pōṭrukirom
punnakai mukhattoḍu puvitannai kāttḍa

O King of the world, we praise You. With Your smiling face You will save the universe!

VIRAHATTIN NOMBARAM (MALAYALAM)

virahattin nombaram uḷḷilotukki ñān
vijanamām dēśam tiraññiṭunnu
māyatan vīthiyil vazhitetti alayunnu
māyā mahēśvari nī nayikku

Holding my grief confined within me, I am searching for an isolated place. I am roaming in the streets of maya, illusion, having lost my way. You are the great goddess of maya. Kindly show me the way!

etranāḷ vēṇḍiṭumammē ivanini
tṛppādadāsanāyi tīrnniṭuvān
nin kṛpā pīyūṣam āsvadippānammē
nin kaṭākṣam ennil patiyēṇamē

How long will it take me to become a servant at Your holy feet? Mother, kindly let your glance fall on me so that I can enjoy the nectar of Your compassion!

śuddha hṛttil vilasunnōrammē – martya
buddhiykkatītamē divya līla
eṅgō maraññu nī rasichiṭunnō - ammē
māyayām kēḷi tuṭarnnīṭumō?

O Mother, You shine in hearts that are pure. Your divine sport is beyond the reach of the intellect. Are You hiding somewhere and indulging in an ongoing play of maya?

rāgādi dōṣam akannīṭuvānennum
hṛttil vasikkumō jagadambikē
nityam bhajikkunnu śraddhayōṭēre ñān
kāruṇyamekū nin paitalinnu

Will You reside in my heart, Mother, so that the blemishes such as attachment are removed? I worship You daily with faith and devotion. Please bestow Your compassion on this child of Yours!

VIRAYARNNARAYĀLTTAḶIRUKAL (MALAYALAM)

virayarnnarayālttaḷirukal kātta
taṭarāṛāyatu pōle
nirmmala hṛdayamulachurasikkumi –
tētoru vātā vēśam?

What special wind is this that delights in agitating our pure hearts, just as tender the leaves of the banyan tree flutter in the breeze?

taruṇaruna kiraṇāvalikanṭāl
ariyām udayam varavāyi
yamunayilōḷam taraḷitamāyāl
ariyām murahari varavāyi!

As the first red rays are sign of the advent of dawn, the ripples on the surface of the Yamuna river announce Lord Krishna's coming!

vanataru pallava vallari kāttil
naṭanacch uvaṭukaḷāṭi rasikke
pozhiyum mazhapōl pūntēn kaṇikakal
pularikkatiroḷi ēttu tilangiḷ

The tender leaves of the forest trees dance in the wind, and drops of nectar falling like gentle rain from the flowers gleam in the dawn's rays.

mādhava mohana muralīravamen
karaḷil kuḷirala pākunnu
ariyātātma hṛdantam sarabhasam
ozhuku, nnonnāyallyunnu!

The captivating sound of Krishna's flute cools my heart. Without my knowing, my heart rapidly flows and dissolves in that bliss.

VIZHITTIṬUVĀY MANAME (TAMIL)

vizhittiṭuvāy maname nam mannanai
anta māya kaṇṇanai saraṇpukuvāy
mukkuṇamum unnai pinni piṇaikkum munne
vizhittiṭuvāy itenna perurakkam

O mind, arise! Please surrender to our king, the mischievous Kannan, who captivates our mind. Before the three attributes entangle you, arise, O mind, from your deep sleep!

saṇcita karma mūṭṭaiyai avizhttu
sakalamum samamāy samaittu koḍuttiḍum
kālattin kōlattil kaṭṭi karittiḍum
kāmamum mōhamum kavarntizhukkum
munne vizhittiṭuvāy itenna perurakkam

Open the bundle of past karmas. In God's creation, there are no differences. Before lust and desire mesmerize you, before being carried away by time, O mind, awaken!

viruppu veruppu ena bhēdamkoṇḍu
onpatu vazhiyil alaintu tirintiṭum
porikaḷ aintilum pukaliṭam koṭutte
vātamum rōgamum vantu māyttiṭu munne –
vizhittiṭuvāy itenna perurakkam

Caught between likes and dislikes, you roam along the nine paths. O mind, arise before you are stricken with the disease of over-indulgence in the five senses.

kālanai tan tōzhanāy koṇḍu
pirappirappu ena pēṇi vaḷarttiṭum
māya ulakil mayanka seyte
tunpattai inpamāy tēḍi kōḍukkum munne –
vizhittiṭuvāy itenna perurakkam

O mind arise! Do not befriend the god Yama, who will ensnare you in the cycle of birth and death through the five senses.

VRAJ MĒ ĀYĀ BASANT (HINDI)

vraj mē āyā basant
par radhā kō barsāt
bhīga hē uskā dāman
āsu bahē dinrāt

Spring has come in Vraja. But Radha only experiences the monsoon season. Tears of seperation from Krisna rain down, day and night, and make Her bosom wet.

jab mēlē mē thē ramē
vraj kē sārē vasī
mathurā kī ōr dēkhē
baithī thī pyārī rādhā

All the residents of Vraja are celebrating the advent of Spring. But Radha is sitting alone, Her gaze fixed towards Mathura, awaiting Lord Krishna.

sunnē kō vō atur
murali kannaiyyā kī
sunī usnē nahī
gīt vō mēlē kī

So anxious is She to hear the sound of Krishna's flute that the music of the festival has no attraction for Her.

'kyun na ayī rādhā'
sakhiyā kehnē lagi
ayēngē jab kānā
tab hē basant mērā

All Her friends wonder – 'Why hasn't Radha come?' Radha says, 'Only when Krishna arrives, will spring arrive for me.'

YĀDUMĀKI NINṬRĀY (TAMIL)

yādumāki ninṭrāy - kāḷī
engum nī niraintāy
tīt nanmaiyellām – kāḷī
deyva līlai yanṭrō?

Kali! You became everything and You are in everything. Are not the bad and good that prevail only the play of God? O Kali!

bhuta maintmānāy – kāḷī
porikaḷaintumānāy
bōdhamāki ninṭrāy – kāḷī
poriyai viṇci ninṭrāy

You became the five elements, Kali, and You became the five senses. You became the awareness, Kali and You became the spirit.

kāḷī mahākāḷī
inpamāki viṭṭāy - kāḷī
ennuḷḷē pukuntāy
pinpu ninnaiyallāl - kāḷī
piritu nānumuṇḍō?

Oh Kali! You have engulfed me as sweetness. After that. oh Kali! It is only You! Do I exist?

anpaḷittu viṭṭāy - kāḷī
āṇmai tantu viṭṭāy
tunpa nīkkiviṭṭāy - kāḷī
tollai pōkki viṭṭāy

Oh Kali! You have bestowed me with love! You have given me the power to rule over myself. Oh Kali! You have removed all my sorrows and troubles.

YAMUNĀ NADI TĪRAM (TAMIL)

yamunā nadi tīram kaṇṇan vizhiyōram
rādhā anurāgam gōpi vaibhōgam

On the banks of the Yamuna river, Krishna is watching. Radha is full of love, the gopis are in bliss.

maunam mozhiyākum manamum mayilākum
kaṇṇan kārmēgham kāṇa mayilāṭum
vizhiyum mozhi sollum vidhiyai atu vellum
kaḷiyil manam tuḷḷum kāttrin idam aḷḷum

(In that environment) silence becomes speech, the mind becomes a peacock who sees the cloud-colored Krishna and dances. The eyes talk, bad karma is destroyed, the mind dances and one feels as if in a soft breeze.

vēṇu isai pāṭum vinaikaḷ parantōṭum
anbil manam kūṭum amaiti tavazhntāṭum
kaṇṇan mukham kāṇa kānti enai īrkkum
sarvvamum avanāka śānti nilaiyākum

Listening to the music from (Krishna's) flute all bad karma disappears, the mind merges in love, a sublime peace reigns. I am pulled as if by a magnet to see Krishna's face and then I feel peace as if everything around is Krishna.

English bhajans

AMALA BHARATAM

ABC 1-2-3, ek do teen India
amala bharatam om
amala bharatam, amala bharatam
amala bharatam om

Mananthavady, Bangaluru, Mysore can't you see?
Amma has come to you dear friends!
We are Her family.
Rise up, clean up, and plant some trees!

O Hyderabad, Pune, Mumbai can't you see?
Amma has come to you, dear friends!
We are Her family.
Rise up, clean up, and plant some trees!

O Amdavad, Jaipur, New Delhi, Zindabad!
Amma has come to you dear friends!
We are Her family.
Rise up, clean up, and plant some trees!

AWAKEN CHILDREN

Awaken children, awaken children.
Awaken to the truth within yourself.

Mother can You hear me, I'm crying out to You.
Alone in this world, searching for something true,
Illusion engulfs me, I'm drowning in ignorance.
How can I find my way home to You again?

How I long to dissolve in Your beauty.
The glory of Your light is all that I would see.
Throwing off the shackles of worldly misery,
I'd find rest in Your love eternally.

Child, won't you rise up from your sleep?
Mother, don't You hear my desperate plea?
Child, aren't you tired of chasing dreams?
Mother, have You not forgotten me?

Can't you hear my voice resounding deep within your soul?
I'm one with you you're not alone.
I can hear Your voice resounding deep within my soul.
You are one with me, I'm not alone.

Awaken children.I hear Your voice calling me back home.
Awaken children. Rejoice in the power of Love.

Awaken children.I see Your light guiding my way home.
Awaken children. Rejoice in the power of Love.

Awaken children.I feel Your spirit lifting me home.
Awaken children. Rejoice in the power of Love.

Awaken children.Truth be told, I'm already home.
Awaken children. Rejoice in the power of Love.

COME RUNNING MY DARLING CHILDREN

Come running my darling children.
Know that Om is your own true nature.
Leaving all sorrow awaken divinity,
Merge in the Self deep within you.

You are the "I" that is in me,
Children, I am the "you" that is in you.
Due to the ignorance, you may feel separate.
In truth there is only oneness.

Bathe in the lake of the Atma
Find the Self that is dwelling withi.n you!
Try to attain and be one with the infinite,
Then you will find bliss eternal.

Just as blue of the vast sky,
And the distant mirage in the desert,
That which is seen is unreal and impermanent.
Be not deceived by illusion.

Mother is walking beside you,
As you stumble and fall on your journey,
Love and devotion, illumine the path ahead,
Holding your hand She will guide you.

EVERYONE IN THE WORLD

Everyone in the world should sleep without fear,
at least for one night, sleep without fear.

Everyone in the world should eat to their fill,
at least for one day, eat to their fill.

There should be one day when there is no violence, no one is injured, no one is harmed.

All people young and old should serve the poor and needy, at least for one day serve selflessly.

This is my dream.this is my prayer.
Love is the answer, love is the way.

HAIL TO YOUR GLORY

Hail to your glory my Lord and my king.
Your life is a story for all hearts to sing,
Your name will protect me I'll come to no harm,
singing Ram Jay Jay Ram Jay Jay Ram Sita Ram.

As I look for shelter, it's never too far.
Your name is my refuge Your name gives me calm.

thinking Ram Jay Jay Ram Jay Jay Ram Sita Ram

As I meet the sorrows and joys of this life,
Your name is my greeting, Your name my goodbye,
saying Ram Jay Jay Ram Jay Jay Ram Sita Ram

As I chose my way at the crossroads at night,
Your name gives direction Your name is my light,
hearing Ram Jay Jay Ram Jay Jay Ram Sita Ram

MOTHER NATURE

Nature is our home,
God in another form.
Let's love and protect, care and respect
The wonder of this world.

Mother Nature,
May our hearts rise in the beauty of creation.

Seeing God in one another
In the wind, the trees, the water.

Every bird that sings, all living things
Are nothing else but you.

As part of the whole we have to play our role,
Learning to feel, striving to heal
The wounds of this world

Nature only gives
Sustaining all that lives
For us to survive we need to strive
To care for all of life

O MIND BECOME SURRENDERED

O mind, become surrendered,
allow only truth to be your friend.
Nobody belongs just to you, no one is your own.

Round and round this world you wander,
not seeing the reason why you're here.
By doing such meaningless actions, you cannot escape.

As you listen to the praises of those who admire all you do,
remember life passes quickly like leaves on a stream.

After being celebrated, this body
that carries you from birth,
will be an abandoned dwelling, forsaken by life.

On and on you struggle bravely,
fulfilling desires of those you love. You sacrifice everything for them, including your life.

Even those who love you dearly
cannot stay beside you after death.

Your body they found so attractive now scares them away.

Captured in the snare of maya,
you're traveling a road that has no end.
Remember the divine Mother, repeating Her Name

Leaving behind all desires,
join in the eternal dance of bliss,
by singing to Mother Kali, Kali Mata.

WE ARE ALL BEADS

We are all beads
Strung on the same thread.
Each one is different,
Yet all are the same.

Love is the thread
That joins us together.
Love is the Essence of
God in us all.

Give your smile to someone lonely.
See it light their face.
In the heart of deepest sorrow
God will shine His grace.

Hold the hand of someone crying.
Shy not from your fear.
Share the burdens of their heart.

Let them know you hear.

Truth can have no country.
Love has no caste or creed.
May the world unite as one.
(By) serving those in need.

YOU HAVE COME TO SACRIFICE

You have come to sacrifice,
You are the candle that burns,
melting down to give us light,
calling us with all your might.

We are just playing around
longing for the things that can't last.
Even then, you won't throw us out,
even when we break your trust.
But time is going by, going by right now,
still we don't know how to use
the candle that burns in front of our eyes.

And all the while, time is going, going by right now.
Still we don't know how to reach You,
the Queen of our heart.

Only you know to where this will lead,
to where we all go, will it be a sad or happy end.
But wherever You go, don't leave me behind,
please don't leave me behind.

Chants

BHAVĀNI BHUJANGAM (SANSKRIT)

ṣaḍādhāra paṅkeruhāntar virājat
suṣumnāntarāḷeti tejōllasantīm
vibantīm sudhāmaṇḍalam drāvayantīm
sudhā mūrtim īḍhe mahānanta rūpām 1

I bow before that personification of nectar, who is the ever lasting immortal bliss, who is the luster in the Sushumna, which is in the six chakras of the body, and who melts the moon and drinks its light.

jvalat kōṭi bālārka bhāsāruṇāngīm
sulāvaṇyaśṛṅgāra śōbhābhirāmām
mahāpadma kiñjalkamadhye virājat
trikōṇōllasantīm bhaje śrī bhavānīm 2

I sing about Bhavani, who sits in the triangle, which shines in the stamen of the great lotus, who has the luster of crores of rising suns, who is immensely pretty, and who attracts the entire world by Her charm.

kvaṇat kiṅkiṇī nūpurō bhāsiranta-
prabhālīḍha lākṣārdra pādāravindam
ajeśācyutādyais-surais-sevyamānam
mahādēvi! manmūrdhni tē bhāvayāmi 3

Oh, great Goddess please keep Your feet, which are adorned with anklets studded with jewels and jingling bells, which shine in the luster of Your wet lac painted feet, and which are worshipped by Vishnu, Brahma and others on my head and bless me.

suśōṇāmbarā badhnī virājan
mahāratnakāñcīkalāpam nitambam
sphurad dakṣiṇāvartanābhiścatisrō-
valīramba! te rōmarājīm bhajeham 4

I worship the streak of hair on Your belly, Thine shining navel circling to the left, Thine hips dressed in red garments, and Your waist adorned with golden tinkling belt, studded with greatest of jewels.

lasat vṛtta muttuṅga māṇikya kumbhō-
pama śrī stanadvantvam ambāmbujākṣi
bhaje dugdha pūrṇābhirāmam tvadīyam
mahā hāra dīptam sadā vismitāsyam 5

I worship Thine twin radiant raised breasts full of milk, which are round and like the gem studded pot, and which are ever brimming with milk, hey Mother who has lotus like eyes.

śirīṣa prasūnōllasad bāhu daṇḍair-
jvalatbāṇakōdaṇḍa pāśānkuśāśca
calatkankaṇōddāma keyūra bhūṣōl-
lasac-chrīkarām bhōjamābāhumīḍe 6

I worship that Bhavani who glitters with Her arms, which are as delicate as Sirisa flowers, and which carry arrow, bow, noose and goad, and which shine with bangles and bracelets.

sunāsāpuṭam patma patrā yatākṣam
mukham devi bhakteṣṭada śrī kaṭākṣam
lalāṭ ōjjvalat gandha kastūribhūṣō-
jvalat pūrṇa candra prabham tē bhajeham 7

With a beautiful nose, long lotus petal eyes, with an auspicious glance that grants the desires of devotees, with a radiant forehead with the smell of musk and shining ornaments, I worship Your face, Devi, which shines like the full moon.

calat kuntaḷānubhramat bhṛmgavṛndair
ghanasnigdha dhammilla bhūṣōjjvalantīm
sphuran mauli māṇikya baddhendurekhā-
vilāsōllasad divya mūrdhānamīḍe 8

I praise Thine head, which is playfully radiant, which is adorned by the crescent moon, which is decorated by the line of gems, in whose dense hair the swarm of bees enter swirl and play, and which is decorated by densely woven white jasmine flowers.

iti śrī bhavānī svarūpam tavaivam
prapañcāt parañ-cāti sūkṣmam prasannam
sphuratvamba! ḍimbhasya mē hṛt sarōje
sadā vāṅmayam sarvatejōmayatvam 9

May this form of Yours, Oh Bhavani, which is much above the universe in its micro form, please shine in the lotus heart of mine, and bless me in Your lustrous form, so that I rule over the wealth of words.

gaṇeśāṇi mādyākhilaiś śakti vṛndaiḥ
sphuracchrī mahā cakra rāje lasantīm
parām rājarājeśvarī traipurīm tvām
śivāṅkōparistham śivām tvām bhajeham 10

I meditate on You, the wife of Shiva, who is sitting pleasantly on His lap, surrounded by Shaktis led by lord Ganesha, who is sitting highly radiant on the chakra raja, and who is Tripura and Rajarajeswari.

tvam arkas tvam agnis tvam āpas tvam indu-
stvam ākāśa bhūr vāyu sarvam tvameva
tvadanyam na kiñcid prakāśōsti sarvam
sadānanda samvitsvarūpam bhajeham 11

I sing about You as a form of blissful knowledge, as one to whom there is none superior, as You are the sun, moon, fire, water, ether, earth, fire and the great essence.

śivastvam gurus tvañca śaktis tvameva
tvamevāsi mātā pitā ca tvameva
tvamevāsi vidyā tvamevāsi bandhur-
gatirme matirdevi sarvam tvameva 12

You are my teacher, You are my lord Shiva, You are the Goddess Shakti, You are my mother, You are my father, You are knowledge, You are my relations, and so You are my only refuge, my only thought, and everything that I can think of.

śrutī nāmagamyam purāṇairagamyam
mahimnānu jānanti pāram tavātra
stutim kartumicchāmi te tvam bhavāni
kṣamasvaivam amba pramugddhaḥ kilāham 13

Though I know not Thine greatness, wish I to praise You, Oh, Bhavani, who is the knower of Vedas and Agamas, and who is unreachable through scriptures. So please pardon me for doing this.

śaraṇyai vareṇyai sukāruṇya pūrṇair
hiraṇyōdarādyai ragaṇyais supūrṇaiḥ
bhavāraṇya bhītaśca mām pāhi bhadre!
namaste namaste punaste namōstu! 14

Salutations, salutations and salutations, Oh Bhavani, You are my refuge, my boon and form of all mercy, You are greatest among all devas, oh holy one, and so, please protect me from this forest snare of life.

bhavānī bhavānī bhavānīti vāṇī
mudārāmudāram mudā ye bhajanti
na śōkō na pāpō na rōgō na mṛtyuḥ
kadācit kadācit kadācinnarāṇām 15

Three times repeat the holy name of Bhavani, with devotion and repeatedly for ever, and get rid of sorrow, passion, sin and fear, for all time and for all ways.

idam śudhacittō bhavānī bhujangam
paṭhan buddhimān bhaktiyuktaśca tasmai
svakīyam padam śāśvatam vedasāram
śriyañceṣṭasidhiñca devīdadāti 16

Who ever correctly reads with devotion, this great hymn praising Bhavani from head to toe, would attain a permanent place of salvation, which is the essence of Vedas, and also get wealth and the eight occult powers.

Index of Bhajans Volume 6

www.ingramcontent.com/pod-product-compliance
Lightning Source LLC
LaVergne TN
LVHW051544080426
835510LV00020B/2849